BT
500

9711

Mendelson
Justices Black
and Frankfurter

KF 8748. M4 1966

DATE DUE

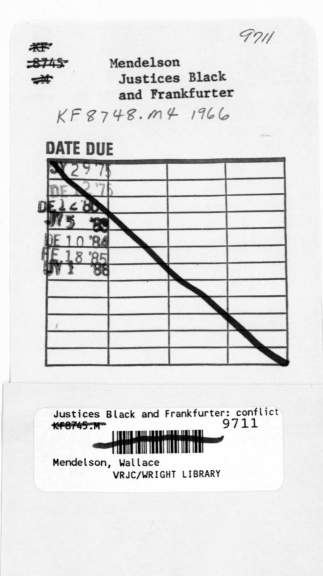

JY 29 '75			
DE 2 '75			
DE 2 '80			
JY 5 '83			
DE 10 '84			
FE 18 '85			
JY 1 '86			

Justices Black and Frankfurter

CONFLICT IN THE COURT

WALLACE MENDELSON

What government is best?
That which teaches us
to govern ourselves.

JOHANN WOLFGANG VON GOETHE

THE UNIVERSITY OF CHICAGO PRESS

CHICAGO & LONDON

Justices

Black

and

Frankfurter:

Conflict

in the

Court

Standard Book Number: 226-51980-5
Library of Congress Catalog Card Number: 61-5781

The University of Chicago Press, Chicago 60637
The University of Chicago Press, Ltd., London

Introduction

... law is always a general statement, yet there are cases which it is not possible to cover in general terms. In matters therefore where, while it is necessary to speak in general terms, it is not possible to do so correctly, the law takes into consideration the majority of cases, although it is not unaware of the error this involves. And this does not make it a wrong law; for the error is not in the law nor in the lawgiver, but in the nature of the case: the material of conduct is essentially irregular.

ARISTOTLE

*T*HE main trouble with the Supreme Court is a general misunderstanding of its role in American government. Without thinking much about such matters, the man in the street assumes that "the law" is crystal clear. He is mistaken. The Constitution comes to us from the eighteenth century. Along with a few later amendments it was written by men wise enough to know they could not prescribe the details of government for an unknowable future. Nor were they in complete accord among themselves on vital issues—just as we are not. And so they often wrote with calculated generality. That is why the Constitution survives while other works of its age—in medicine, engineering, and every other field—have long since passed away. The Founding Fathers, like the amenders, avoided strait-jacketing precision. Their forte was the suggestive, open-ended hint. Not unlike the Delphic oracle, their "meaning" usually depends upon the wisdom of those who contemplate their words.

Even modern legislation is full of ambiguity. Congress dealing merely with present problems on a year-to-year basis cannot anticipate all the eventualities of life. Nor are congressmen, more than the rest of us, known for unanimity on even those issues which they can foresee.

Of course in many contexts the law is clear. To the extent that this is true there is little litigation. What controversy there is will seldom reach the Supreme Court. Cases which go that far generally do so precisely because the law with respect to them is cloudy—and precisely because they involve not a clash of right and wrong, but of competing rights.

That each state shall have two senators is too plain to require judicial interpretation. But what is the meaning of such constitutional terms as "due process of law," "commerce among the several states," or "equal protection of the laws"? These and other basic constitutional phrases have, and doubtless were designed to have, the chameleon's capacity to change their color with changing moods and circumstances. This is why they survive in a world their authors never knew. Short of constitutional amendment, we leave the final burden of "interpreting" such elastic terms to the Supreme Court. This means we expect the judges to solve for us many of the great dilemmas of life. For surely it is plain by now that the old eighteenth-century document does not automatically provide solutions for Atomic Age problems. And so the crucial question is: Where shall the Court find guidance when the light of the law fails? Shall it be past decisions—however out of date? Shall it be the good sense, or moral aspirations of the community, or perhaps natural law? And how may these be ascertained? If none of them, alone or in combination, what then?

We assume, or perhaps we are taught, that somehow the ancient parchment contains within its four corners the answers to all problems. *We* of course cannot read them there, but judges are supposed to have some special vision. Yet, each of

us seems convinced that, if a decision does not coincide with
his own emotional preference, then the judges must be biased,
or worse. The Constitution is infallible, but judges are not—
unless they happen to agree with us.

Sooner or later, if our system is to thrive, Americans must
recognize that neither the Constitution nor any other legal code
provides plain answers to most of the great issues that divide
us. Soon or late we must acknowledge that cases which go as
far as the Supreme Court usually represent conflicts between
highly commendable principles none of which can fully prevail in life on earth. Each is apt to have impressive legal backing. In such conflicts "the law" is far from clear. Yet judges
must somehow decide cases. They must solve enigmas that no
other agencies of government, nor we ourselves, have been able
to solve. This is a fearful responsibility. What Samuel Butler
called "the art of life" is also the jurist's art: "to derive sufficient conclusions from insufficient premises."

Until we have a better understanding of the Supreme
Court's real function, that institution will be in trouble. For
just so long an important element of free government will be in
danger. The purpose of this little book is to explore the nature
of the judge's job. If the emphasis is upon the work of Justices
Black and Frankfurter, that is not because they must be accepted as "heroes." It is rather that they represent with uncom-
mon ability two great, if differing, traditions in American jurisprudence. Eventually, perhaps, we will have to choose between
them.

Lest anyone suffer embarrassment by association, I forbear
from mentioning the names of those who gave me the benefit
of their counsel on the manuscript—after all, I had the final
word. And so I go no farther than to acknowledge a deep in-
debtedness for their wise and gentle help.

I also acknowledge with thanks the kind permission of the
copyright holders to reproduce passages from the following
publications:

Harvard Law Review, for an item from "Mr. Justice Jackson," by Louis Jaffe, which appeared in *68 Harv. L. Rev.* (1955).

Massachusetts Law Quarterly, for a selection from "The Contribution of an Independent Judiciary to Civilization," by Learned Hand, which appeared in *The Supreme Judicial Court of Massachusetts, 1692–1942.*

New Republic, for passages from "Can the Supreme Court Guarantee Toleration?" by Felix Frankfurter, which appeared in the *New Republic,* June 17, 1925.

Alfred A. Knopf, Inc., for passages from John P. Frank's *Mr. Justice Black, The Man and His Opinions* (1949).

Passages from Arthur Sutherland's *The Law and One Man among Many* (1956) are reprinted with the permission of the copyright owners, the Regents of the University of Wisconsin, and the University of Wisconsin Press.

Edith Bolling Wilson and Columbia University Press have given me permission to quote from Woodrow Wilson's *Constitutional Government in the United States* (1908).

Contents

1 THE DEPRESSION, HITLER, AND THE LAW

> We do not realize how large a part of our law is open to
> reconsideration upon a slight change in the habit of the
> public mind.
>
> OLIVER WENDELL HOLMES

*T*HE Civil War was a hotbed for American industry. It
proved the potentialities of the factory system and produced
large pools of liquid capital. It also freed government from
bondage to the southern planters. The result was an industrial
revolution. Between 1860 and 1900 capital invested in manufacturing increased tenfold—finally surpassing that devoted to
agriculture. Railroad trackage jumped from 30,000 to 193,000
miles. Edison harnessed electricity; Bell produced the telephone; and Ford was developing the mass-produced automobile. By 1899 the first gargantuan trust—the Standard Oil
Company—had been created. Its founder, John D. Rockefeller,
observed that "The day of combination is here to stay. Individualism is gone never to return." Or, as Bernard Baruch put it,
private initiative had merged into corporate collectivism. In
1904 Moody listed 318 "greater or lesser" trusts. A few years
later the Pujo Committee reported that J. P. Morgan and associates held directorships in 112 corporations with combined
assets greater than the assessed value of all property west of the
Mississippi River.

Along with these developments came revolutionary changes
in basic law. We kept the old Constitution but boldly tailored
its meaning to accommodate the new era. Beginning in the
1890's, "laissez-faire" economic ideals (which some judges
had been advocating for a generation) became the law of the

land. A new theory of states' rights—called Dual Federalism—arose to defeat national regulation of "private enterprise."[1] For all their "rights" the states too lost a great measure of control over business.[2] This was accomplished largely by reading a substantive, i.e., "laissez-faire," meaning into the Due Process clause of the Fourteenth Amendment. These and related innovations gave the captains of industry broad freedom to develop the nation's vast natural wealth—without the watchful hand of government to protect the common man from exploitation.

By 1900 the newly contrived labor injunction doomed workmen's efforts at self-help,[3] just as Dual Federalism and Substantive Due Process undermined his efforts to secure protective legislation.[4] Midwestern agrarian attempts to block the worst abuses of the industrial revolution were also checkmated by the judiciary. Emasculation of the Interstate Commerce Commission left the railroads free to continue their extortionate practices without national—or state—interference.[5] Trusts obtained a large measure of immunity from prosecution[6] and thanks to a Court decision their ill-got income was tax-exempt.[7] Invalidation of the income tax as an alternate source of federal revenue undermined hopes for tariff reform. Thus the consumer—farmer and laborer—was saddled with the cost of monopoly and the cost of government. Even Andrew Carnegie recognized, *after he retired*, that labor, unorganized and without legislative protection, was "helpless against capital." Farmers, selling in a competitive world market and buying in a trust-dominated, tariff-protected, domestic market, were similarly handicapped.

The synthesizing force behind these economic and constitutional developments was a new philosophy for a new industrial America. It found cogent expression in the life and writings of Andrew Carnegie, the most articulate nabob of the economic revolution. Carnegie of course did not originate the "Gospel of Wealth," he merely epitomized the spirit of his era:

> We of the capitalistic persuasion put trust in the individual man. We make him a part, according to his particular skill,

of a great and far-reaching industrial organization. We demote him when his ability fails, and discard him if we find a serious flaw of character. In our system there is nothing, save his own shortcomings, to prevent his rising from the bottom to the top. We have, then, a method, better than that of practical politics, for selecting the leaders of a democracy. By a process of pitiless testing we discover who are the strong and who are the weak. To the strong we give power in the form of the autocratic control of industry and of wealth with which the leader, who has thus risen by a process of natural selection, can and does do for the masses of the community what they could never do for themselves. We agree with Alexander Hamilton that the voice of the able few should be equal to, nay, greater than that of the mediocre many in the actual government of society. So we demand that the political State shall leave us alone. We have little faith in the State as a constructive agency and less in it as an efficient instrument. The politician is a slave to the whims of the masses, a master of favoritism for his own ends, and a waster of the public substance. We demand of the State protection of property. For this purpose we ask an adequate police, a sound banking system, a sound currency based on gold, and court decisions to nullify social legislation confiscatory in character. We demand a tariff to protect us against our foreign competitors and a navy to guard our commerce and our stakes in other lands. When the State has fulfilled these, its proper functions, we ask it to leave us alone. We point to the progress already achieved under laissez faire. We guarantee that, if our conditions are met, the sun of prosperity will fill the land with light and happiness.[8]

The effectiveness of a philosophy or a myth, of course, does not depend upon its truth or internal consistency. Only radicals questioned the compatibility of frontier ideals and industrial enterprise; of "individualism as a pattern of belief and the corporation as a pattern of control." Only the hypersensitive resented the harnessing of America's moral aspirations to the service of materialism. Few but outsiders wondered how aggressive, individual, self-concern could bring social harmony. All this, along with more tangible abuses by the great tycoons, was irrelevant. The important thing was that the Gospel of

Wealth worked. It inspired generations and produced economic goods in kind and quantity beyond belief. Buttressed with huge supplies of raw material, and free of old-world social strictures, it all but solved man's oldest problem: shortage of the necessities and amenities of life. If the cost came high in broken lives, perverted traditions, and moral insensitivity, the achievement also was great.

Yet ultimately the Gospel of Wealth failed—less from its side effects than from a defect of its genius. Preoccupied with production for monetary gain, it neglected the problem of distribution. More accurately, perhaps, its opulence created that problem. Distributive techniques inherited from ages of poverty were obsolete in an era of mass production. As Brooks Adams saw it, the industrial revolution had "evolved under the stress of an environment which demanded excessive specialization in . . . money-making. . . . To this money-making attribute all else had been sacrificed. . . ."

Despite "artificial" restraints upon production which Veblen lampooned in *The Engineers and the Price System*, goods piled up periodically beyond the market's ability to absorb. Some saw in this the nub of the business "boom and bust." In any case when the old order collapsed in the Great Depression its stoutest defenders found the fault in "overproduction"—while a third of the nation was "ill-housed, ill-fed, and ill-clothed." Brooks Adams no doubt would have blamed overspecialization. The modern Keynesian diagnosis was "oversaving": a choking accumulation of funds that found no outlet either in consumption or creative investment. This idle money meant idle men and idle markets. Under earlier, mass-poverty conditions it may have been a safe assumption that savings automatically became productive capital. Experience in an opulent, mass-production economy taught a different lesson. Though funds were available, businessmen were not anxious to expand plant capacity in the face of "oversupplied" consumer markets.[9] Idle money went into the stock market and real estate. Unemployment at one end of the economy and "speculation" (read gambling) at the other mounted to a crisis.

The New Deal revolution and much that followed was an experiment in the problem of distribution, of finding ways for the Common Man to acquire the vast goods that industry knew how to produce.[10] Madison Avenue and installment credit for consumers had not sufficed. Responding to the spirit of the new times, the Roosevelt judges *unanimously* discarded the constitutional innovations of the 1890's. "Laissez faire" and its legal props, Substantive Due Process, Dual Federalism, etc., had served their purpose. America had learned the secret of mass production. Other problems now pressed for solution.

Under the most friendly of governments industry had choked itself into stagnation. How could the economy be saved, how buttressed against the future, without legislation? Conditions being new, legislation would have to proceed on a trial-and-error basis. Government, both state and national, needed freedom to experiment. This the new Supreme Court provided by discarding the restraints of economic "laissez faire." The judicial response, in short, was not a blind reaction to crisis but an affirmative contribution to the needs of the day. "If the people," said Judge Charles E. Clark,

> are not in command of their own government, but are actually subordinate to some yet more remote sovereign who upholds and justifies unsanitary conditions, long hours of labor and general defiance of social welfare as a freedom required by some vague constitutional command or higher [gospel], then we are nearer either anarchy or the rule of the autocratic few than we are democracy.[11]

But the domestic economy was not the only problem of the 1930's. Our tranquillity was challenged from another quarter. This was the heyday of dictators. Germany, Japan, Italy, and Russia had recovered sufficiently from World War I to contemplate aggression—territorial and ideological. Democracy itself was under attack. In the age of the Gestapo and the O.G.P.U., the Bill of Rights and the Civil War amendments assumed new luster. Again the Constitution responded to the impact of the times. Having mastered mass production, America turned from the special interests of businessmen to the general interests which all men have in common: a more bountiful enjoyment of civil liberty and the fruits of industrial know-how.

Judicially prescribed "laissez faire" is a thing of the past. The Supreme Court is no longer the constitutional arbiter of economic policy. That function has been returned to legislative bodies and the people to whom they must answer. In this something old has been restored. We have returned to Chief Justice Marshall's vision of national power[12] and Chief Justice Waite's respect for state authority.[13] But there have been innovations, too, at least in emphasis. Allowing so much to the political processes, the Court has been especially concerned for their purity. Hence the stress on free speech, press, assembly, and religion; fair governmental procedures; and freedom from racial discrimination. Behind all this lies that deep regard for the whole human personality—with its thirst for growth and self-expression—which is the foundation of Democracy: respect, that is, for Everyman without special concessions for economic man.

Such was the response of our judicial system first to the crisis of industrial revolution and then to the Great Depression and the Age of Dictators. The old Constitution-symbol survives in a world of change because, thanks in part to the Supreme Court, it responds to the life around it. Each generation contributes its gifts. What remains useful survives as basic law. The rest is sloughed off from crisis to crisis. If in the wisdom of hindsight the old Court erred, the error was not in responding affirmatively to the dominant, "laissez-faire" spirit of the age. This is inevitable for living institutions. The fault, rather, if such it may be called, lay in perpetuating an attitude (or myth) that had outlived its usefulness. But in this the Court erred no more than many, perhaps most, Americans and most American institutions. In 1933 President Hoover's Research Committee on Social Trends reported after an elaborate survey that

Social institutions are not easily adjusted to inventions. The family has not yet adapted itself to the factory; the church is slow in adjusting itself to the city; the law was slow in adjusting to dangerous machinery; local governments are slow in adjusting to the transportation inventions; international relations are slow in adjusting to the communication inventions; school curricula are slow in adjusting to the new occupations which machines create. There is in our social organizations an institutional inertia, and in our social philosophies a tradition of rigidity. Unless there is a speeding up of social invention or a slowing down of mechanical invention, grave maladjustments are certain to result.

We turn now from the background of the new jurisprudence to some of its inherent difficulties. To free *both state and national authority* from outmoded "laissez-faire" restraint is to enlarge the area of potential conflict between them. To release national power is to complicate the relation between the President, Congress, and the courts. To respect and foster civil liberty is to quicken an old enigma: at what point does liberty degenerate into license, or freedom into chaos? And so the Court's constant quandary is how and where to strike a balance between state and national competence; between presidential, congressional, and judicial authority; between the claims of the individual and those of society. Each of these is a problem in the relation of a whole to its parts. Each springs from a basic postulate of American government: Federalism; the Separation of Powers; Democracy. Behind each is a broader problem in the division of governmental authority: to what extent shall answers be provided by the judicial, and to what extent by the political, processes?

For issues of such magnitude there is no ready solution either in the written Constitution or in the life that sustains it. Answers come by trial and error. Logic, as Holmes taught, is not the chief force in the growth of the law. The purpose of the chapters that follow is to trace the impact of two great minds upon the new Court's struggle with these problems. *Our concern is not so much with the merits of decisions as with what*

is more readily demonstrable: the directions of judicial think-
ing and the role of the Supreme Court in American society.
Our central figures are Justices Hugo Black and Felix Frankfurter. They have been the polar forces on the new Court—and
spokesmen for two contending traditions in our jurisprudence.

In many respects the two men have much in common. Each
sprang from a background as unpromising as that of Abraham
Lincoln. Each has devoted his talent to public service. Both are
deeply democratic in the Jeffersonian sense. They are more
sensitive, that is, to interests which all men have in common
than to the special interests of businessmen. Hamiltonianism is
not for them. Theirs is the liberal tradition of Jefferson, Jackson, Lincoln, Wilson, and the Roosevelts. Yet as judges their
views are diametrically opposed. They disagree as to the
nature of the judge's job and his role in American government.
But the things they stand for respectively are not idiosyncratic.
They reflect old traditions and residues of ancient conflict.
What is unusual is that two such powerful protagonists have
sat together for so long with colleagues so evenly divided between them. Generally the Court oscillates from one view to
the other. Yet neither has ever prevailed completely. While one
dominates, the other normally finds expression in futile dissent; futile at least for the moment. The difficulty of the
Court is that in the crisis of our time it has been torn—like the
rest of us—between two great traditions. But this rift wears a
jewel in its head. Never before on the bench has the role of the
Court in our federated democracy been canvassed with such
outspoken, intellectual vigor. Here perhaps posterity will find
unique greatness in the "new" Supreme Court.

2 THE SEPARATION OF POWERS: GOOD NEIGHBOR POLICY

The makers of our federal Constitution followed the [Separation of Powers] as they found it expounded in Montesquieu, followed it with genuine scientific enthusiasm. The admirable expositions of the Federalist read like thoughtful applications of Montesquieu to the political needs and circumstances of America. They are full of the theory of checks and balances. The President is balanced off against Congress, Congress against the President, and each against the courts. Our statesmen of the earlier generations quoted no one so often as Montesquieu, and they quoted him always as a scientific standard in the field of politics. Politics is turned into mechanics under his touch. The theory of gravitation is supreme.

The trouble with the theory is that government is not a machine, but a living thing. It falls, not under the theory of the universe, but under the theory of organic life. It is accountable to Darwin, not to Newton. It is modified by its environment, necessitated by its tasks, shaped to its functions by the sheer pressure of life. No living thing can have its organs offset against each other as checks, and live. On the contrary, its life is dependent upon their quick cooperation, their ready response to the commands of instinct or intelligence, their amicable community of purpose. Government is not a body of blind forces; it is a body of men, with highly differentiated functions, no doubt, in our modern day of specialization but with a common task and purpose. Their cooperation is indispensable, their warfare fatal. There can be no successful government without leadership or without the intimate, almost instinctive, coordination of the organs of life and action. This is not theory, but fact, and displays its force as fact, whatever theories may be thrown across its track. Living political

9

constitutions must be Darwinian in structure and in practice.

Fortunately, the definitions and prescriptions of our constitutional law, though conceived in the Newtonian spirit and upon the Newtonian principle, are sufficiently broad and elastic to allow for the play of life and circumstance. Though they were Whig theorists, the men who framed the federal Constitution were also practical statesmen with an experienced eye for affairs and a quick practical sagacity of the actual structure of government, and they have given us a thoroughly workable model. If it had in fact been a machine governed by mechanically automatic balances, it would have had no history; but it was not, and its history has been rich with the influences and personalities of the men who have conducted it and made it a living reality. The government of the United States has had a vital and normal organic growth and has proved itself eminently adapted to express the changing temper and purposes of the American people from age to age.

WOODROW WILSON

*N*OWHERE are the differing approaches of Justices Black and Frankfurter more starkly revealed than in the *Steel Seizure* case.[1] To avert an industry-wide strike during the Korean conflict, President Truman seized the steel mills. Admittedly Congress had provided quite different ways for dealing with such crises. Government lawyers argued that in meeting the emergency the President had acted "within the aggregate of his constitutional powers as . . . Chief Executive and . . . Commander in Chief." Mr. Justice Black spoke briefly for the Court. The seizure could not be justified as an exercise of military power. Then, noting Congress' *refusal* to authorize what the executive had done, the Justice found it forbidden by the Separation of Powers: "In the framework of our Constitution, the President's power to see that the laws are faithfully executed refutes the idea that he is a lawmaker. . . . And the Constitution is not silent about who shall make laws which the President is to execute."

Apparently Mr. Justice Black found the meaning of the Constitution so obvious that no judicial or other precedents need be examined. It was simply a matter of "deducing" an inevitable conclusion from a major premise: the Separation of Powers. No troublesome qualifications were recognized.

All other members of the Court found the problem more complex. Even the concurring judges wrote supplemental opinions. What troubled them was a minor premise that Mr. Justice Black ignored: both history and the Constitution sharply qualify the Separation of Powers as an element of American government. If Article I of the Constitution gives Congress legislative power, Article II gives the President a veto. This may be exercised on the *legislative* ground that the congressional measure is not acceptable policy. It may rest on the *judicial* ground that Congress has acted illegally. So too, while Article III vests "the judicial power of the United States" in federal courts, Article I puts the power to try impeachments in the Senate. For these and kindred provisions the Founding Fathers were charged with violating "the maxim that the legislative, executive, and judicial departments ought to be separate and distinct." Madison's response in *The Federalist*, No. 47, is a confession and avoidance. Our system is not one of separated powers but of separated branches each having some measure of legislative, executive, and judicial authority. The result is "checks and balances."

Even what remains of the Separation of Powers has been qualified by American experience since 1789. The dissenters in the *Steel Seizure* case noted an impressive array of presidential "lawmaking." Without waiting for Congress, Washington proclaimed neutrality; Adams warranted Robbins' arrest; Jefferson bought Louisiana; Monroe issued his famous doctrine; Jackson removed government deposits from the Bank of the United States; Lincoln emancipated the slaves; and so on, down through Truman's venture in sending troops to Korea.

Mr. Justice Frankfurter agreed with the Court's decision, but "the considerations relevant to the legal enforcement of the . . . separation of powers [seemed to him] more complicated and flexible than may appear from what Mr. Justice Black has written." So too, he rejected the historical effort of the dissenters; "It is as unprofitable to lump together in an undiscriminating hotch-potch past presidential actions claimed to be [inherently authorized], as it is to conjure up hypothetical future cases." Then he carefully defined the issue lest past decisions and customs be gratuitously undermined, or the future unnecessarily hemmed in:

> We must . . . put to one side consideration of what powers the President would have if there had been no legislation whatever bearing on the authority asserted by the seizure, or if the seizure had been only for a short, explicitly temporary period, to be terminated automatically unless Congressional approval were given. These and other questions, like and unlike, are not now here.

He then proceeded to the crucial issue:

> The powers of the President are not as particularized as are those of Congress. But unenumerated powers do not mean undefined powers. The separation of powers built into our Constitution gives essential content to undefined provisions in the frame of our government.
>
> To be sure, the content of the three authorities is not to be derived from an abstract analysis. The areas are partly inter-acting, not wholly disjointed. The Constitution is a framework for government. Therefore the way the framework has consistently operated fairly establishes that it has operated according to its true nature. Deeply embedded traditional ways of conducting government cannot supplant the Constitution or legislation, but they give meaning to the words of a text or supply them. It is an inadmissibly narrow conception of American constitutional law to confine it to the words of the Constitution and to disregard the gloss which life has written upon them. In short a systematic, unbroken, executive practice, long pursued to the knowledge of the Congress and never before questioned, engaged in by Presidents who have also sworn to uphold the Constitution, making as it were such exercise of power part of the structure of our government, may be treated as a gloss on "executive power." . . . Such was the case of *United States* v. *Midwest Oil Co.*, 236 U.S. 459. The

contrast between the circumstances of that case and this one
helps to draw a clear line between authority not explicitly
conferred yet authorized to be exercised by the President and
the denial of such authority.

In the case referred to, public lands which Congress had
opened for entry had been temporarily closed by executive
order as in 252 prior instances over a period of eighty years.
The Justice could find no comparable tradition of executive
seizure—the narrowly limited history of which he reviewed in
detail. Here is the careful technician recognizing both sides of
the case—the minor as well as the major premise; cautiously
limiting his issue lest more than enough be decided; proceed-
ing inductively when he feels compelled to recognize that tradition has given contour to principle; and openly revealing the
rational steps from issue to judgment.

Beginning with the same Separation premise Mr. Justice
Black arrived at the same result. What happened in between
was quite different. He recognized nothing that might taint the
pristine simplicity of the Separation of Powers. Mr. Justice
Black understands the power of the elemental. His characteristic tools are the great, unquestioned verities. He draws no
subtle distinctions. The niceties of the skilled technician are
not for him. His target is the heart, not the mind. His forte is
heroic simplicity. His opinions attain great power because they
seldom bother with mundane considerations that baffle others—
e.g., application of a winged principle in a less than ideal
world; or the impingement of one vast Platonic truth upon
another. In a word, Mr. Justice Black is an idealist. His wisdom
is the wisdom of the great idea. He knows with Chesterton that
"the center of every man's existence is a dream." He insists
that we live up to our highest aspirations—and when we fail to
do so he would save us from ourselves. Finally, it will appear,
his idealism is deeply colored (some might say compromised)
by sympathy for what the New Deal called the "forgotten
man." In contrast, Mr. Justice Frankfurter is a pragmatist. His
wisdom is the wisdom of experience. His forte is reason, not

14

hallowed bias or noble sentiment. He has little confidence in the capacity of judges to sit in judgment upon the community, to erase its errors—if such they be. He counts more on man's ability to learn than to be taught. In the absence, then, of unusually compelling circumstances he accepts our compromises with eternity as the essence of the law—and leaves us free to grow with experience; to learn the lessons that come with self-inflicted wounds.

THE MEANING OF CONGRESSIONAL MEASURES

In government, too, form follows function. Legislative power is parceled out along with political responsibility, while the judicial function of applying general law to concrete cases belongs to those who are "independent" of political pressure. This is implicit in the Separation of Powers. The hitch is that while legislative and judicial functions are distinct at their cores, their outer boundaries inevitably overlap. Lawmaking is not an exact science. Legislation is largely a compromise between Utopia and the status quo—and reason is seldom the key to compromise. Nor is human foresight equal to the legislator's job. Like the rest of us, he cannot anticipate all the implications of his policy. The common language in which statutes must be written is less than precise; play must be allowed for contingency for the future is packed with surprise.

The legislator, then, cannot provide specifically for every circumstance within the general ambit of his purpose. This inability must be made good by judges when the unforeseen arises in a concrete case. And so the legislative and judicial functions legitimately overlap. As Learned Hand has put it:

> . . . a judge is in a contradictory position; he is pulled by two opposite forces. On the one hand he must not enforce whatever he thinks best; he must leave that to the common will expressed by the [legislature]. On the other hand, he must try as best he can to put into concrete form what that will is, not by slavishly following the words, but by trying honestly to say what was the underlying purpose expressed.[2]

But, given this limited entree into the policy domain, judges sometimes go further. The line between the licit and illicit is vague at best. Even for the most detached, the temptation to find one's hopes or fears in the "purpose" of a statute must be very great. Above all, our bench and bar are trained in the tradition of the common law whose judges in fact were law-makers. Inevitably that heritage colors this and other aspects of American government, including the legislative process itself. Today, Supreme Court cases not resting on legislation are all but nil. It follows that statutory construction is at or near the heart of the modern judicial process.

Holmes's remark that "the meaning of a sentence is to be felt rather than . . . proved" expressed the truth that interpretation is an act of judgment. "When we talk of statutory construction we have in mind cases in which there is a fair contest between two readings, neither of which comes without respectable title deeds. [The reading of a law] can seriously bother courts only when there is a contest between probabilities of meaning."[3]

Behind all the other difficulties is the cardinal fact that legislation, being essentially a compromise between conflicting views, must often speak in something less than logically compelling terms. This is the judge's dilemma. But far more than a mere matter of lawyer's technique is involved. We are told that "the legislative way of life" is the essence of freedom under government.

> Legislation is a process slow and cumbersome. It turns out a product—laws—that rarely are liked by everybody, and frequently little liked by anybody. . . . [W]hen seen from the shining cliffs of perfection the legislative process of compromise appears shoddy indeed. But when seen from some concentration camp of the only alternative way of life, the compromises of legislation appear but another name for what we call civilization and even revere as Christian forbearance.[4]

In short, by the give-and-take of the legislative process we achieve an equilibrium of interests as the foundation for social peace. The alternative, at least until philosophers become kings, is suppression of dissent by might, myth, and money in the fashion of the dictators.

If social compromise is the essence of legislation, what is the true nature of the judicial function in the construction of statutes? Learned Hand suggests the answer:

> [P]rovided that the opportunity always exists to supplant [laws] when there is a new shift in political power, it is of critical consequence that they should be loyally enforced [by judges] until they are amended by the same process which made them. That is the presupposition upon which the compromises were originally accepted; to disturb them by surreptitious, irresponsible and anonymous [i.e., judicial] intervention imperils the possibility of any future settlements and pro tanto upsets the whole system. *Such laws need but one canon of interpretation, to understand what the real accord was.* The duty of ascertaining its meaning is difficult enough at best, and one certain way of missing it is by reading it literally, for words are such temperamental beings that the surest way to lose their essence is to take them at their face. Courts must reconstruct the past solution imaginatively in its setting and project the purposes which inspired it upon the concrete occasions which arise for their decision.[5]

These generalities are brought to earth in a series of Supreme Court interpretations of the Fair Labor Standards Act (FLSA) and the Federal Employers' Liability Act (FELA). As introduced to the Senate in 1937 the embryo of FLSA invoked the full scope of Congress' commerce power for the regulation of wages and working hours. Indeed, as Attorney General (later Mr. Justice) Jackson pointed out in committee, the bill "combines everything, and is an effort to take advantage of"[6] every generous interpretation of the Commerce Clause then known, whether expressed in majority or dissenting opinions. After running the gauntlet of opposition by the United States Chamber of Commerce, the National Association of Manufacturers, the National Publishers Association, the National Association of Wood Manufacturers, the Cotton Textile Institute, and the Anthracite Institute, among others,[7] the measure emerged in much compromised form. Full use of the commerce power had been abandoned in favor of coverage only for employees "engaged in [interstate] commerce," or "in the production of goods for [interstate] commerce," with the gloss that "an employee shall be deemed to have been engaged in the production of goods if such an employee was employed . . . in any process or occupation necessary to the production thereof, in any state." In short, full recourse to the "Shreveport" doctrine and related broad constructions of national power had evaporated. Something less than all enterprises, or all workers, *"affecting"* interstate commerce were covered. On the other hand, Congress had gone part way along the "affectation" road by including not only workers in interstate commerce but also those engaged in jobs "necessary" to production of goods for such commerce.

It required no great imagination to foresee that the latter provision would cause trouble. How much had Congress meant to include? What jobs are, and what are not "necessary to the production of goods" for interstate trade? How far back in the chain of causation do these words carry? Speaking through Mr. Justice Frankfurter, the Court had little difficulty in finding that maintenance employees of a loft building leased out for the manufacturing of goods for interstate trade were protected by FLSA.[8] Only Mr. Justice Roberts of the old guard dissented. Even maintenance workers in the separate office building of a producer for "interstate" commerce were held to be covered, although here two members of the Court dissented.[9] But what of maintenance men in a typical, general office building leased to a great variety of enterprises, including executive and sales offices of manufacturing and mining concerns? Here Mr. Justice Frankfurter, for the Court, drew the line.[10] Congress plainly had not exercised the full scope of its power. In construing the phrase "necessary to . . . production" of goods for commerce, the Justice said:

> We must be alert . . . not to absorb by adjudication essentially
> local activities that Congress did not see fit to take over by
> legislation. Renting office space in a building exclusively set
> aside for an unrestricted variety of office work spontaneously
> satisfies the common understanding of what is local business.
> . . . Mere separation of an occupation from the physical
> process of production does not preclude application of the
> . . . Act. But remoteness . . . is a relevant factor in drawing the
> line. Running an office building as an entirely independent
> enterprise is too many steps removed from the physical process
> of the production of goods. Such remoteness is insulated from
> the . . . Act by those considerations pertinent to the federal
> system which led Congress not to sweep predominantly local
> situations within the confines of the Act.

Justices Black, Douglas, Murphy, and Rutledge thought otherwise. They found controlling significance, evidently, in a literal
reading of the word "necessary" in the crucial coverage clause.

Surely, neither position is demonstrably true or false. But
some such distinction as Mr. Justice Frankfurter made was
inevitable if Congress' compromise between the exercise of all
or none of its commerce power was to be respected. Moreover,
any line that the Court might draw would be dialectically vulnerable, as such lines always are, when judged exclusively by
bordering cases. Surely it is significant that while four Justices
thought the Court had not gone far enough, two thought it had
gone too far.[11] As a matter of hindsight it may be noted that
in 1949 Congress approved Mr. Justice Frankfurter's distinctions. To stabilize the principle behind them it deleted the
cryptic "necessary to . . . production" clause and substituted
"directly essential to . . . production."

In *Vermilya-Brown* v. *Connell*[12] the question was whether
FLSA applied to an American military base in Bermuda. The
law had been enacted in peacetime with no contemplation of
such a problem. It did, however, by express terms cover our
"possessions," i.e., presumably Alaska, Hawaii, Puerto Rico,
Guam, the Samoan Islands, the Virgin Islands, and the Canal
Zone. Mr. Justice Black was with a majority which held the act

applicable—without regard for the practical implications of injecting American wage standards far into the economy of a friendly, foreign sovereign. Mr. Justice Frankfurter was one of four dissenters who rejected such an expansive approach. They thought the decision gave FLSA an effect which Congress surely had not foreseen. The result would embarrass our foreign relations.

That more than disagreement as to the meaning of words is involved in these cases is suggested in the pattern of disagreement over other provisions of the same act. The original bill had prohibited child labor in comprehensive language. But, unlike the fate of the original wage-hour provisions, this was not just watered down; it was eliminated. Instead, Congress substituted a prohibition on the "shipment" in interstate commerce of "any goods . . . produced in an establishment" employing children. Western Union admittedly used children as messengers, but claimed exemption because it was not a "producer of goods." The act defined "produce" to mean "produce, manufacture, mine, handle, or in any other manner work on. . . ." The Court, including Mr. Justice Frankfurter, agreed that telegraph messages were "goods" as defined in FLSA. But it could not find that Western Union was a "producer" of, or that it "shipped," messages.[13] To bring such a company within the act would require "a series of interpretations so farfetched and forced as to bring into question the candor of Congress as well as the integrity of the interpretative process. . . . To translate this act . . . into an equivalent of the bills Congress rejected is, we think, beyond the fair range of interpretation." Here, too, Justices Black, Douglas, Murphy, and Rutledge disagreed.[14]

The same pattern of disagreement may be seen in decisions under the "engaged in commerce" provision. All of the Justices agreed, for example, that a cook who prepared meals for maintenance-of-way employees of a railroad was not engaged in the production of goods for interstate trade, or in a related process or job. But was he "engaged in commerce"? The Court thought not. This clause, it said, "covered every employee in the 'chan-nels of interstate commerce' . . . as distinguished from those who merely affected that commerce."[15] Justices Black, Douglas, Murphy, and Rutledge again dissented. They could not believe that Congress had used its powers more "sweepingly" with respect to "production" than with respect to "activities . . . in transportation or connected therewith. . . ."[16]

Of all the forms which legislative compromise may take, the most difficult is that which simply bypasses vital issues. Some-times congressional failure to face a problem is a conscious passing of the buck to judges. Often, perhaps, it is oversight. What shall the Court's guide be in such an impasse? FLSA provides:

> No employer shall . . . employ any of his employees . . . for a work-week longer than forty hours . . . unless such employee receives compensation for his employment in excess of [forty hours] at a rate not less than one and one-half times the regular rate at which he is employed.[17]

Congress apparently had not considered how this principle should be applied in the case of longshoremen who usually do not work steadily for one employer, but shift from one to an-other, often daily, as employment opportunities are offered. For some twenty years prior to FLSA, this problem had been handled by collective bargaining agreements whereby long-shoremen were paid "straight time" during specified daylight working hours and "overtime" for week-end and night work. With the acquiesence of employers, labor union, and govern-ment, this practice was continued after enactment of the wage and hour law. A few workers, about one in a thousand, did sometimes work more than forty hours per week for a single employer. Rejecting their own union's collective bargain, they instituted an action for double damages under the act, assert-ing that night and week-end work had been so common in their employment that the contractual "straight time" pay could not be deemed their statutory "regular rate" of pay. Rather, they argued, such "regular rate" was the average received for all their work from any one employer including both "straight time" and "overtime." This claim was upheld by the Court.[18]

Had Congress meant to provide "overtime" on "overtime" in this manner? Had its purpose been to disturb a long-established, collectively bargained method of handling overtime pay in an industry whose work habits were necessarily too irregular to fit readily into the common pattern? Mr. Justice Frankfurter, joined by Justices Jackson and Burton, thought the Court had gone too far. For him nothing in the statutory term "regular rate" required a technical construction divorced from the habits and usage of the industry. Moreover, he noted, Congress had rejected the Portal-to-Portal decisions[19] involving a related problem. In so doing Congress observed pointedly that FLSA had been "interpreted judicially in disregard of long-established customs, practices, and contracts between employers and employees," to the detriment of industrial peace. Here, the Justice thought, the Court was repeating the same mistake which Congress had found it necessary to undo in the Portal-to-Portal Act. Again, as in the cases referred to, Mr. Justice Frankfurter's dissenting views were vindicated by subsequent act of Congress. The same is true of his dissent from the Court's view that FLSA precludes bona fide settlement of genuine disputes on overtime pay and damages even where the employees were given the overtime compensation in full.[20] There too his position had been that

> [for] purposes of judicial enforcement, the "policy" of a statute should be drawn out of its terms, as nourished by their proper environment and not, like nitrogen, out of the air. Before a hitherto familiar and socially desirable practice is outlawed [the court should have] at least . . . a broad hint [from Congress].

The pattern suggested by these cases shows up more boldly in statistical terms. From its first decision in 1941 through June, 1959, the Court gave full-dress opinions in fifty-nine FLSA cases.[21] Except in four[22] where the issues were simple enough to be settled unanimously, Mr. Justice Black voted consistently "prolabor." Mr. Justice Frankfurter upheld workmen's claims in thirty-two, and employer claims in twenty-seven. Black apparently read FLSA in the spirit of its sponsors' aspirations. Frankfurter seemingly saw the same language in the light of more earthbound considerations—industrial traditions and the amorphous, yet very real, compromise which Congress had struck between the hopes of FLSA's friends and the fears of its opponents. It will be noted that with respect to at least four different cases, the expansive views of Mr. Justice Black were repudiated by Congress in favor of the more moderate position which Mr. Justice Frankfurter and others had found implicit in the original measure.

Unlike FLSA, the Federal Employers Liability Act (FELA) is an "old deal" measure. A workman is entitled to compensation for an industrial accident only if he proves negligence on the part of his employer, a costly and often difficult procedure. More modern state workmen's compensation acts reject the negligence approach in favor of an insurance, or absolute liability, principle. They provide, in effect, that industrial accidents are part of the cost of production and must be paid for by industry just as it pays other operating costs. Congress has been urged to adopt the modern view, but it has refused to do so. Negligence is still the heart of FELA.[23] Mr. Justice Frankfurter is constantly pointing out that while this is "outmoded and unjust," it is the law and as such should be respected. The harshness of the old approach, however, may be mitigated if the Supreme Court is prepared to review the evidence *in cases where the lower courts have found no liability*. This raises another problem. Should the highest court of the land review cases which turn on nothing more than an appraisal of evidence on *the inevitably unique circumstances* of each particular accident? Or should the nation's ultimate court conserve its time and energy—as it is permitted to do—for *legal* problems of *general* significance? After all there are thousands of negligence cases each year. The Supreme Court could not possibly review all of them. Each turns on its own peculiar facts. Since the same events do not repeat themselves, a decision in one case rarely, if ever, has precedent-value for another. Such litigation does not present or settle any disputed question of law. The problem, rather, is the application of established rules of negligence to an endless series of new circumstances. Surely such matters, involving unique and private claims, are the responsibility of the U.S. Courts of Appeals and the state appellate tribunals. The Supreme Court's responsibility is larger. Of the scores of thousands of cases decided each year it can review only a handful. Congress has authorized it to select that handful on the basis of general importance to the nation's legal system—not because of the importance to an individual litigant. Chief Justice Hughes explained this authoritatively as follows: "If further review [beyond that in the lower appellate courts] is to be had by the Supreme Court, it must be because of the public interest in the question involved. . . . Review by the Supreme Court is thus in the interest of the law, its appropriate exposition and enforcement, not in the mere interest of the litigants."[24] Thus, for example, a classic entree to the high court is for the purpose of settling constitutional issues or resolving conflicts between lower courts. A prime consideration in such cases is uniformity of federal law throughout the nation. This synthesizing and rationalizing function is something which only the Supreme Court can achieve, for it is the only common denominator of our fifty state (and eleven federal) appellate court systems. Here is more than enough to occupy nine supreme judges.[25] Moreover, to give favored treatment to any particular class of litigants such as FELA plaintiffs would seem improper in view of the Court's responsibility to other litigants and the public.

Does all this amount to saying that we can have justice in general without having it in the concrete case? And is justice, or simply law enforcement, the high court's function? Mr. Justice Frankfurter's response may be implicit in these observations from the famous *Wilkerson* case:

> Considering the volume and complexity of the cases which ob-
> viously call for decision by this Court, and considering the
> time and thought that the proper disposition of such cases
> demands, I do not think we should take cases merely to review
> facts already canvassed by two and sometimes three courts even
> though those facts may have been erroneously appraised. The
> division in this Court would seem to demonstrate beyond perad-
> venture that nothing is involved in this case except the draw-
> ing of allowable inferences from a necessarily unique set of
> circumstances. For this Court to take a case which turns
> merely on such an appraisal of evidence, however much hard-
> ship in the fallible application of an archaic system . . . may
> touch our private sympathy, is to deny due regard to the con-
> siderations which led the Court to ask and Congress to give
> power to control the Court's docket. Such power carries with it
> the responsibility of granting review only in cases that de-
> mand adjudication on the basis of importance to the operation
> of our federal system; importance of the outcome merely to
> the parties is not enough.[26]

The Justice then observes that the principle at stake cannot
be appreciated in the perspective of a single case:

> Despite the mounting burden of this Court's business, this is
> the thirtieth occasion in which . . . *certiorari* has been granted
> during the past decade to review a judgment denying recovery
> . . . in a case turning solely on jury issues. The only petition
> on behalf of [an employer] that brought such a case here
> during this period was dismissed. . . .

There follows a broad hint as to who was responsible: "Of
course some light on the situation is derivatively shed by the
disclosed position of the Justices on the merits of the cases."
That light reveals surprising data. In twenty-one Terms of
Court (1938–58) more than sixty FELA decisions turned upon the sufficiency of evidence.[27] Save in one case where plaintiff on the witness stand had all but repudiated his own claim,[28]
it does not appear that Justices Black or Douglas ever voted
against a workman. Justices Murphy and Rutledge voted with
similar consistency prior to their departure in 1949, as have
Chief Justice Warren and Mr. Justice Brennan more recently.

Thus during most of his tenure Mr. Justice Black has had three staunch supporters. This is especially significant because it requires only four votes (via *certiorari*) to bring cases of this type before the Court.[29] Once a case is there other judges (unlike Mr. Justice Frankfurter since 1949) feel compelled to vote on its merits.[30] In this manner a determined four will often pick up a random fifth vote (or more). The net result, it seems to some, is that by its generosity in finding possible fault on the part of employers ". . . the Supreme Court has in effect converted this negligence statute into a compensation law thereby making, for all practical purposes, a railroad an insurer for its employees."[31] To put it differently, no four judges are willing to impose the alien chore of negligence litigation upon the Supreme Court for the benefit of employers. There are four who often do so at the instance of workmen—*over sustained dissent on* certiorari *grounds*. It follows that employers do not get an added chance to win their cases, but employees frequently do.[32]

Two recent decisions illuminate these problems. In *Cahill* v. *New York, New Haven and Hartford Rd.*,[33] a brakeman had been assigned temporarily to direct traffic at a grade crossing. He stopped a line of automobiles because the road was partly blocked by a train but he allowed traffic to proceed in the opposite direction. While standing between the waiting vehicles and the train, the brakeman turned to watch the progress of the moving traffic. As he did so a truck which he had halted moved forward and injured him. He sued the railroad, contending that the injury was *caused by its failure to instruct him in traffic control*. The U.S. Circuit Court of Appeals found that negligence had not been proved and that if the railroad was at fault, as charged, that fault was not the cause of the accident. The Supreme Court reversed without opinion. Justices Reed, Frankfurter, Burton, and Harlan thought the case should not have been reviewed. A few months later, in a most unusual move, the Court recalled its judgment as erroneous. Chief Justice Warren, and Justices Black, Douglas, and Clark dissented.[34]

The outcome in *Moore* v. *Terminal Railroad Association*[35] was more typical. There a *per curiam* opinion of three sentences reversed the Missouri Supreme Court for rejecting a jury verdict of negligence. Mr. Justice Harlan concurred reluctantly. Mr. Justice Frankfurter thought the case should not have been reviewed. Mr. Justice Burton joined his brother Whittaker in dissent as follows:

> In my view the record does not contain any evidence of negligence by respondent, but instead it affirmatively shows that the sole cause of petitioner's injury was his own negligent act. Hence, I think the Supreme Court of Missouri was right in holding that there was nothing to submit to a jury.

> The undisputed facts, principally physical facts, are these. Respondent's tracks run in pairs to the south from a point just outside the waiting room of its Union Station in St. Louis. Between each pair of tracks is a concrete loading platform designed for the use of passengers in walking, and of respondent's employees in transporting baggage, to and from trains. The platform between tracks numbered 4 and 5 is the scene of this occurrence. It is about 18 inches high, 14 feet 1⅜ inches wide and 1,800 feet long. It is under a roof supported by metal posts 14 inches in diameter located down the center of the platform at 30-foot intervals. At the time of this occurrence a train was standing on track 4 abutting the west side of the platform, and an incoming train was being backed north toward the waiting room along the east side of the platform on track 5. Petitioner, who was employed by respondent as a baggage handler, was on this platform for the purpose of transporting baggage from the incoming train. He was using a hand cart, referred to in the evidence as a "flat wagon," which was 14 feet 8 inches long (including the handlebars at either end), 3 feet 8 inches wide, and supported in the center by an axle riding on two 26-inch wheels, operating both as a fulcrum and a pivot. Being some distance south of the point at which the baggage car was to be stopped for unloading, petitioner started pulling his cart to the north along the east side of the platform and adjacent to the moving train. After so proceeding a short way, he observed a 4-wheel wagon standing on the east side of the platform, slightly north and east of one of the roof supports, making it necessary for him to turn his cart to the left and to

pass on the west half of the platform. At that time another hand cart, a few feet to the left and ahead of him, was also being moved to the north over the west half of the platform. In changing the course of his cart, petitioner pulled its north end to the west at such an angle as caused its south end to be pivoted and swung to the east against the third car of the moving train which, in turn, caused him to be thrown to the west against a car standing on track 4 and to be injured. Other wagons were on the platform but were either some distance behind or ahead of petitioner and had no connection with this occurrence.

It cannot be, and is not, denied that the casualty resulted solely from the collision of the cart with the moving train. What caused this to happen? Petitioner admits that it was the turn of the cart that did so. He also admits that the turn was made by his own hand. How then may it be said that any act of respondent caused or contributed to cause the south end of the cart to collide with the moving train? Petitioner attempts to attribute his conduct in some way to the presence of the other hand cart which was being pulled to the north a few feet ahead and to the west of him, saying that except for its presence he "could have made that turn easy." Yet he admits not only that there was no contact between that cart and his, but also that it was moving ahead and away from him. Surely the presence of that moving cart at that place did not constitute negligence. Do not these admitted and indisputable physical facts show that the casualty was not one "resulting in whole or in part from the negligence of" respondent? Do they not show that the casualty was one "resulting in whole" from the negligence of petitioner? The Federal Employers' Liability Act does not create liability without fault. Liability under the Act is predicated on both negligence and causation. By the plain words of § 1 of the Act a railroad is made liable for injuries to its employees "*resulting* in whole or in part from [its] *negligence.*" (Emphasis added.) 53 Stat. 1404, 45 U.S.C. § 51, 45 U.S.C.A. § 51. "The Act does not make the employer the insurer of the safety of his employees while they are on duty. The basis of his liability is his negligence, not the fact that injuries occur. And that negligence must be 'in whole or in part' the cause of the injury." Ellis *v.* Union Pacific R. Co., 329 U.S. 649, 653. . . . I submit that the simple facts recited do not show even a "scintilla" or an "iota" of evidence, to say

> nothing of any substantial evidence, of negligence by respondent. Instead, I insist, they affirmatively show that it was petitioner's own act in turning the cart at such an angle as brought its south end into collision with the moving train that was exclusively "the cause of the injury."
>
> To hold that these facts are sufficient to make a jury case of negligence under the Act is in practical effect to say that a railroad is an insurer of its employees. Such is not the law. For these reasons I dissent.

Surely, if what was proved in these cases may be treated as culpable negligence, that concept has acquired new dimensions. Doubtless judges who take the expanded view do so in response to the modern emphasis upon security. The customary concept of negligence—in whose image FELA was adopted—reflects the frontier ideal of individualism. Under it each man was responsible for his own welfare and answerable to no one except for clear, direct, and personal fault. The more modern trend, emphasizing the interdependence of men in industrial society, expects some operations to insure their risks regardless of fault. Should courts recognize this trend and "interpret" statutory law accordingly, or should they wait for legislation? Obviously Justices Black and Frankfurter respond differently to this problem.

The *Moore* case illustrates another facet of the sixty-odd FELA cases that concern us here. The Missouri Supreme Court had repudiated the jury finding of negligence as beyond the realm of reason. For years state and federal judges have exercised such authority when in their view the evidence in a case plainly points in one direction. The thought is that a jury's function is to decide between competing claims *when the evidence is in substantial conflict*. But when a court is satisfied that reasonable men could find only one way, it may take the case from the jury. This is a safeguard against runaway verdicts. Experience teaches that in contests between unfortunate plaintiffs and "rich" corporate defendants, juries tend to follow their sympathies, not the evidence. *Moore* and related

FELA cases come to the Supreme Court on the charge that the courts below erred in taking them from juries. Some effort has been made to justify Supreme Court intervention on right-to-jury grounds.[36] But no one questions that right in these cases. Conversely, no justice has questioned the judicial duty to take an FELA case from a jury when the evidence leaves no room for doubt.[37] Thus we are back to the basic problem: appraisal of the peculiar evidence of each unique industrial accident. If the crux of the FELA cases really is trial by jury, why is it that the same principle, similarly invoked in other litigation, does not bring a comparable number of cases to the Supreme Court?[37a]

It is worth passing notice that when the interests of a forlorn criminal-case defendant may be served by rejecting jury findings, Mr. Justice Black seems somewhat less concerned for the sanctity of trial by jury than he purports to be in the FELA cases.[38] And is it not strange that in admiralty litigation in which there is no right to trial by jury his voting record in favor of employee-plaintiffs matches his record in the FELA cases?[38a] Moreover, if the Justice is generous with *discretionary* review at the request of injured workmen, he has been a bit miserly with appeals *as of right* involving *legal* issues presented by businessmen. Indeed he has repudiated, as too "frivolous" for Supreme Court adjudication, business claims which every one of his associates has found worthy of adjudication.[39] These "inconsistencies" are more formal than real. In each instance the Justice is on the "liberal" side, the side of the "common man" (worker and consumer vis-à-vis the businessman) and the forlorn criminal-case defendant. Mr. Justice Black's sensitivity to workmen's claims in the FELA and FLSA cases is surpassed only by his consumer-sensitivity in antitrust litigation. In ten years (1949–59) the Court reached decision on Sherman Act "monopoly" issues in nineteen clashes (direct or indirect) between business and consumer interests.[40] Only Mr. Justice Black found a violation of the law in every instance.

Other decisions involving other legislation might be examined, but the differing approaches of Justices Black and Frankfurter in the cases discussed are typical. For one a generous "New Deal" humanitarianism seems to be decisive. The other, as judge, is more concerned with the basic distinction between legislative and judicial functions, lest the freedom of the people to govern themselves, well or badly, be hampered by judicial "legislation."

STATUTES AND STARE DECISIS

A peculiar problem in construction arises when the Supreme Court is called upon to reconsider its own earlier reading of a legislative measure. Abstractly, nothing more is involved than a simple application of the principle of *stare decisis*—let past decisions be respected. But suppose those decisions had evoked powerful dissent by such men, perhaps, as Holmes, Brandeis, and Stone? Suppose, too, that in the interim a shift in political power had been reflected on the bench, the new judges having gone to school, so to speak, to the great dissenters? Our premise, of course, is that the legislature has not seen fit to alter the statute in question, though perhaps it had been urged to do so. Such is the background of *Girouard* v. *United States*.[41] Three earlier decisions flatly held that Congress had denied naturalization to persons otherwise qualified who refused on pacifist grounds to bear arms. Building upon great-name dissents in the earlier cases, Justices Black, Douglas, Rutledge, Murphy, and Burton held that the former decisions "did not [reflect] the correct rule of law," nor was there crucial significance in the fact that Congress, though persistently urged to do so, had not changed its ways.

Girouard's case is particularly interesting because Chief Justice Stone, who (as Associate Justice) had been one of the great dissenters in a crucial earlier case, now had a chance to correct the "mistake." But he did not take the opportunity. Three decisions of at least fifteen years' standing, refusal by six successive Congresses to make vigorously urged changes, and, finally, re-enactment of the same provisions were as decisive for him as for Justices Frankfurter and Reed.

Mr. Justice Frankfurter's position in *Girouard* does not turn solely upon the very special "legislative history" which the dissenters there emphasize. His deep respect for established decisions is seen in case after case where no comparable evidence of congressional "adoption" is available. The Justice's position simply is that the long-settled judicial construction of a statute, and established doctrines which have grown up around a statute, are part of the statute itself. Alteration then is a matter for the legislature. As one of his famous predecessors said, it is usually not so important that a law be "just," whatever that may mean, as that it be settled; for stability and and predictability themselves are important elements in a healthy legal system. Moreover, "judicial legislation" of this type entails serious problems of retroactivity.

Accordingly, Mr. Justice Frankfurter (unlike Black) could not accept a reinterpretation of the Mann Act which would save polygamists from its penalties;[42] nor a departure from precedent that altered railroad liability under the Carnack Act;[43] nor disregard of an ancient doctrine which prevented an assigner from raising the invalidity of his patent against the assignee;[44] nor violation of a settled definition of "unseaworthy";[45] nor abandonment of long-established principles of negligence law where Congress has made "negligence" the test of liability for purposes of the Federal Employers' Liability Act;[46] nor departure from a settled construction of legislation concerning the reviewability of Interstate Commerce Commission orders denying reparations.[47] The crux of the Justice's position in these cases is suggested in the following:

> Of course the law may grow to meet changing conditions. I do not advocate slavish adherence to authority where new conditions require new rules of conduct. But this is not such a case. The tendency to disregard precedents in the decision of cases like the present has become so strong in this Court of late as, in my view, to shake confidence in the consistency of decision and leave the courts below on an uncharted sea of doubt and difficulty without any confidence that what was said yesterday will hold good tomorrow. . . .[48]

A related problem arises when the Court is asked to reconsider an interpretation of the Constitution after Congress, meanwhile, has acted in the light of the former decision. Such, in substance, is the *South-Eastern Underwriters* case.[49] For seventy-five years the Court had held that the "business of insurance is not commerce" within the meaning of the Constitution.[50] Twenty-one years after the beginning of that line of cases, Congress, in the Sherman Act, penalized restraints of interstate commerce. More than half a century later our problem came up. Had Congress penalized restrictive, interstate, insurance transactions? Justices Black, Douglas, Murphy, and Rutledge held in the affirmative, and theirs was the prevailing view, for Justices Roberts and Reed did not participate. Chief Justice Stone with Frankfurter and Jackson dissented. For them it seemed plain, in the words of Mr. Justice Frankfurter, that Congress, by adopting the Sherman Act,

> . . . did not mean to disregard the then accepted conception of the constitutional basis for the regulation of the insurance business [by the states]. And the evidence is overwhelming that the inapplicability of the Sherman Act, in its contemporaneous setting, to insurance transactions such as those charged by this indictment has been confirmed and not modified by Congressional attitude and action in the intervening fifty years.

There is a revealing difference in the attitude of the dissenters on the constitutional and the statutory questions involved. All agreed that the facts of business life had brought at least some aspects of the insurance business within the regulatory power of Congress. To confine or side-step a constitutional decision that has become an anachronism is one thing; to force that "reversal" retroactively upon an unsuspecting Congress is something quite different. Congress can amend legislation with relative ease. The people may choose a new Congress. But amending the Constitution is a cumbersome process (subject to "veto" by a minority).

Helvering v. *Griffiths*[51] raises a similar problem. In 1920 the Court had held that stock dividends were not constitutionally taxable as income, Justices Holmes, Brandeis, Day, and Clarke dissenting.[52] Thereafter, in 1936, for other purposes, the Court distinguished between different types of stock dividends, holding that some did constitute income in the constitutional sense.[53] Then Congress amended the revenue laws to include as taxable income all corporate dividends excepting such as do "not constitute income within the meaning of the [Constitution]." A majority found in the legislative history of that provision a congressional purpose simply to include within its coverage such dividends as the 1936 decision permitted. The dividends in the principal case, not being within that category, were immune.

A large part of the legislative history in support of the Court's position came from the remarks of Senator Hugo Black. *Justice* Black, along with Justices Douglas and Murphy, dissented. Mr. Justice Rutledge did not participate. In the minority view, Congress had not meant merely to go as far as possible while honoring *both* the 1920 and 1936 decisions. Rather, Congress had sought instead to "reverse" the 1920 decision—a reversal which the dissenters were willing to sustain. If, as the Court intimates, Mr. Justice Black was less willing to compromise on a liberal cause in the one forum than Senator Black was in the other, that is a fair reflection, as has been suggested, of a difference between the judicial and legislative processes.

Although there is truth in the suggestion that every problem of construction is unique, a pattern seems evident in these cases. In all nine of them Mr. Justice Frankfurter adhered constantly to the principle that changes in established interpretations of legislative policy are matters for Congress. At the other extreme, only Justices Black and Murphy consistently bypassed precedent, thereby achieving a more liberal legislative result. While Justice Rutledge did not participate in one case, only once did he and Justice Douglas differ with Black and Murphy. This involved the lost cause of polygamy.

Ironically, a case in which Mr. Justice Frankfurter found circumstances justifying a departure from precedent has brought him perhaps more criticism than any other venture. This was *United States* v. *Hutcheson*,[54] a criminal prosecution under the Sherman Act growing out of a labor union's "secondary boycott." Doubtless many sponsors of the Clayton Act (labor's so-called magna charta) thought that measure had freed such boycotts from the taint of crime. But the *Duplex* decision[55] in 1921 at least implied otherwise. Mr. Justice Frankfurter, for the Court, recognized that controversial case as relevant, unless Congress, meanwhile, had nullified it. Admittedly, Congress had not done so explicitly, but the Justice found that "the Norris-La Guardia Act has expressed the public policy of the United States . . . in terms that no longer leave room for doubt" as to the legislative liquidation of *Duplex*. It followed that Hutcheson could not be convicted. Mr. Justice Black was part of the majority which supported this view.

Critics urge that the Norris-La Guardia Act had nothing whatever to do with the criminality of any conduct but only with the jurisdiction of federal courts to issue labor injunctions. Some of Mr. Justice Frankfurter's remarks (when separated from the balance of what he says) invites this attack. But the Justice would hardly be so naïve as to turn his case on the untenable proposition that foreclosure of federal injunctive relief ipso facto precludes federal prosecution. This part of his argument must be read in conjunction with what precedes and follows it. The Justice's position is simply that, alone, section 20 of the Clayton Act clearly would immunize Hutcheson's conduct from injunction and criminal prosecution under the Sherman Act. The *Duplex* decision, however, by strained construction of the term "labor dispute," had destroyed the immunity from injunction and thereby raised questions as to the immunity from prosecution. Thereafter, Congress had rejected *Duplex*. As the House Committee on the Judiciary put it:

> The purpose of the [Norris-La Guardia] bill is to protect the rights of labor in the same manner the Congress intended when it enacted the Clayton Act . . . which act, by reason of its construction and application by the Federal courts, is ineffectual to accomplish the congressional intent.[56]

The crux of the matter is that in the Clayton Act, and again in the Norris-La Guardia Act, Congress defined the concept of a legitimate "labor dispute" in terms broad enough to protect the *Hutcheson* type of activity, while *Duplex* defined that crucial legislative term more narrowly. Mr. Justice Frankfurter accepted the congressional rather than the *Duplex* definition. To be sure, the Norris-La Guardia redefinition occurred in a purely anti-injunction context—*the only context in which the old court had erred*. But the fact that Congress fashioned the remedy to fit the precise "mistake" which the Court had made did not, in Mr. Justice Frankfurter's view, detract from its primary purpose, as the House Judiciary Committee said, to "protect the rights of labor in the same manner the Congress intended when it enacted the Clayton Act. . . ." Mr. Justice Frankfurter's critics read the Norris-La Guardia "intent" narrowly, in the light of the remedy which it afforded. Thus, for them, while Congress clearly wanted to kill *Duplex* injunctions, it simultaneously wanted the *Duplex* definition to live on as the authoritative interpretation of the Clayton Act in criminal matters. Perhaps so, but certainly Congress did not say this in explicit terms. On the contrary, the Norris-La Guardia preamble is plainly broad enough to embrace what the House Judiciary Committee deemed to be the purpose of that measure: rejuvenation of Clayton. Indeed the preamble is broad enough to introduce section 20 of the Clayton Act itself. This, no doubt, is why Mr. Justice Frankfurter referred particularly to the preamble when he said that Congress in the Norris-La Guardia Act had "explicitly formulated the 'public policy of the United States' in regard to industrial conflict, and by its light established that the allowable area of union activity was not to be restricted, as it had been in the *Duplex* case. . . ." In this view Congress had uprooted all, not just a part, of the *Duplex* error.

The difference between Mr. Justice Frankfurter and his critics is that he found the key to Norris-La Guardia in its broad preamble; they find it in the relatively narrow provisions which outlaw labor injunctions. Doubtless the Justice and his associates would have been on safer ground if they had let the specific prevail over the general.

One suspects that Justices Black and Frankfurter were on the same side of this controversial case for quite different reasons. The former perhaps simply voted as usual—in accordance with the labor-prone pattern of his record in the FLSA, FELA, admiralty, and NLRB cases.[57] His colleague apparently was willing to find so much in Norris-La Guardia because there is so little guidance in the Sherman Act, a measure enacted fifty years before to deal with the old problem of business trusts. Judicial efforts to adapt it to the new problem of labor unions had been somewhat less than brilliant. Thus *Hutcheson's* case raised a teasing problem in the Separation of Powers. Should the Court rest upon *stare decisis;* should it try to improve upon its past, improvident lawmaking—or should it withdraw and let Congress provide at least some hints for what was then, clearly, *the beginning of a new era in labor history?* If in the face of this dilemma Mr. Justice Frankfurter "legislated" with uncharacteristic boldness (by reading too much into the Norris-La Guardia Act), he did so apparently because the alternative was to devise, piece by piece, a new code of labor antitrust law. At best, perhaps, it was a matter of legislating a little to avoid legislating a lot. The net result was that the Court rejected and turned back to Congress responsibility for the fashioning of national labor law.

ADMINISTRATIVE AGENCIES AND THE RULE OF LAW

In perspective, the ability of the Anglo-American legal system to accommodate changing social needs has been one of its major merits. But in the short view such accommodations are often painful. In a few generations we have had to assimilate change from frontier to industrial life; from competition to oligarchy in large segments of the economy; from "laissez faire" to the service state. The inadequacy of traditional governmental procedures in the face of this challenge produced the modern administrative process. When, for example, it was recognized that we could not rely upon competition to regulate railroad rates, governmental regulation became inevitable. But the old system of judicial enforcement of legislative mandates was not adequate for the task. Legislatures discovered that rate regulation involved subtleties beyond their competence. Their universal response was to delegate such problems to specialized administrative agencies—which had, or could be expected to develop, techniques commensurate with the esoteric nature of the work assigned to them.

At first the courts refrained from interference. They, too, seemed to recognize that what constituted "fair and reasonable" railroad rates was a problem for specialists. But such scruples soon yielded to "laissez faire." By the end of the nineteenth century, the judiciary had made itself, in effect, the supervisor of the new regulatory system. To give administrative specialists the final word on railroad and utility rates was deemed incompatible with fundamental property rights. For judges to take upon themselves responsibility for such matters constituted that much desired goal, the "rule of law." The judiciary thus became a bottleneck in the very system that had arisen to make good the inadequacy of the judicial and legislative processes in the face of new problems.

A judiciary freed of its early psychotic hostility surely has much of value to contribute to this modern development in the machinery of democratic government, but its inherent institutional handicaps are not to be discounted. Judges cannot maintain an uninterrupted interest in a relatively narrow area of socioeconomic activity. They must, of necessity, be jacks-of-all-trades. They cannot initiate litigation but must await the sporadic pleasure of plaintiffs. When cases do arise, issues and records are fixed by the litigants for their own ends, which may or may not coincide with public needs. The judicial process is slow and costly. Rate cases, for example, are apt to become moot before they can run the long course of judicial review. Above all, the crucial issues before administrative tribunals are seldom legal issues. Nor can they, as our experience demonstrates, be converted into legal issues by dressing them up in lawyers' jargon.

> The determination of utility rates [for example]—what may fairly be exacted from the public and what is adequate to enlist enterprise—does not present questions of an essentially legal nature in the sense that legal education and lawyers' learning afford peculiar competence for their adjustment. These are matters for the application of whatever knowledge economics and finance may bring to the practicalities of business enterprise.[58]

Judicial hostility towards the administrative process died with the fall of the "nine old men." Mr. Justice Frankfurter marked the beginning of a new attitude when, speaking for the Court, he observed that the administrative and judicial processes are not to be deemed rivals but "collaborative instrumentalities of justice and the appropriate independence of each should be respected by the other," to the end that modern economic problems may be solved without sacrifice of ancient liberties.[59]

Generally speaking, Congress has divided authority between the judicial and administrative processes in the following manner. An administrative agency is created to deal with a particular area of problems in accordance with general standards laid down by legislation. It is authorized to hold hearings and issue regulatory orders on the basis of its findings. By act of Congress administrative findings of fact are final (if supported by substantial evidence). But findings of law are subject to judicial review. This simply recognizes the expertise of the administrative agency with respect to facts within its domain, while courts are deemed to be expert in law. Each, then, has final authority within its specialty. The teaser is that the line between a finding of fact and a finding of law is not always clear. The question of whether a given railroad rate is "fair and reasonable," for example, cannot easily be broken down into its constituent legal and factual elements. The two blend into one another without a break. In John Dickinson's classic diagnosis a generation ago, "It would seem that when the courts are unwilling to review, they are tempted to explain by the easy device of calling the question one of 'fact,' and when otherwise disposed, they say it is a question of law."[60] This was the old approach that served so well the interests of "laissez faire."

For Mr. Justice Frankfurter, "expertise"—comparative competence—is the touchstone for reconciling administrative discretion and "the rule of law." It follows that administrative findings must stand unless they are based on clear mistakes of law. Mr. Justice Black seems satisfied to leave recondite matters for those who are specially competent to deal with them—unless the results offend his liberal tenets. The crux of the matter is seen in E. M. Dodd's study of National Labor Relations Board orders reviewed by the Court during a crucial four-year period (1941–45). The board was successful in seventeen out of twenty-one cases. The record, Professor Dodd concludes, "demonstrates that the Supreme Court is now insisting that circuit courts of appeals must give the Board a free hand to administer its statute, with a minimum of judicial interference not only with respect to its findings of fact, but also with respect to its rulings on questions which are on the border line between law and fact and with respect to its discretionary power to devise such remedies as it may consider appropriate. This judicial attitude is explicable to some extent as a specific application of a general tendency to limit judicial interference with administrative agencies in their performance of the duties which the legislature has imposed upon them. But it is clear that the Board's string of victories has not been due solely to the Supreme Court's general attitude toward administrative agencies. For a majority of the members of the Court—and particularly Justices Black, Douglas, Murphy, and Rutledge, the Justices who have been the most unwilling to set aside anything which the Labor Board has done—have during the same four terms of court shown considerably less reluctance to reverse the Interstate Commerce Commission, an administrative agency at present somewhat out of favor in so-called liberal circles."[61] During the period in question, ICC orders were sustained in only nine out of sixteen cases. That respect for the administrative process was more compelling for Mr. Justice Frankfurter and that regard for a "liberal" agency was more weighty for Mr. Justice Black is suggested by their contrasting positions in these two groups of cases. Mr. Justice Black voted to sustain the NLRB in twenty out of twenty-one instances, the ICC in only two out of fifteen. The percentages are approximately ninety-five and thirteen respectively.[62] Mr. Justice Frankfurter, on the other hand, voted to sustain the NLRB in sixteen out of twenty-one cases and the ICC in thirteen out of sixteen. Here the percentage figures are roundly seventy-six and eighty-one respectively. In a similar later period (1953–57), Mr. Justice Black favored the ICC in two out of ten cases,[63] the NLRB in only eight out of eighteen.[64] If the Justice's attitude in the one area remained constant, in the other it seems to have changed. The Taft-Hartley Act—to say nothing of the Eisenhower Administration—had intervened.

Behind all this litigation lies the perpetual problem of reconciling general principles of law and human needs in special situations. As John Frank has said,

> People are not made for courts, but courts for people; and yet a court sitting at the top of a great ladder, deciding only a few cases a year chosen on the basis of their general importance, must keep its eye on the whole picture as well as on the particular case. . . . If a court focuses only on the particular people before it, it may do justice in a particular case and yet make very poor general policy; and so it is often said that hard cases make bad law. On the other hand, if a court . . . concentrates overly much on little specialties of practice or procedure, then the court has become precious, or overly finicky, too much interested in itself to serve the general good.[65]

It is only a surface paradox that Mr. Justice Black, the idealist, concentrates heavily on the outcome of the immediate case—whereas his pragmatic associate is deeply concerned that law be the same for all persons; that basic legal changes must come from legislation, not from judges. In the FELA, FLSA, and early NLRB cases, Mr. Justice Black is able to make three quite different legal principles—*certiorari*, statutory construction, and the rule of law—yield a common "prolabor" result. For, however different the *legal* contexts in which these cases arise, they are all incidents in the so-called struggle between labor and capital. Obviously, sympathy for one side or the other is less decisive for Mr. Justice Frankfurter than the distinctive and generally recognized legal considerations by which he measured each of the three different problems. If his *certiorari* position in the FELA cases leads to sharply "conservative" results, his insistence on administrative law principles in the 1941–45 NLRB cases brought markedly "liberal" results. His constructions of FLSA on the other hand have been more nearly middling.

For Mr. Justice Black, plainly the essence of law is Justice—as he sees it. And he sees it with benign sensitivity to the plight of the "needy." The result is that a legal principle—*certiorari*, for example—is apt to mean one thing when "liberal" interests are at stake and something quite different with respect to "conservative" claims. In contrast, the essence of law for Mr. Justice Frankfurter is regularity and uniformity. To emphasize these—along with neutrality as the crux of the judicial function—and to leave the other elements of Justice largely to the lawmaking branches of government is to emphasize the Separation of Powers.

3 DEMOCRACY: WHAT BELONGS TO CAESAR AND FROM WHAT MUST CAESAR ABSTAIN?

Is a legal concept a finality, or only a pragmatic tool? Shall we think of liberty as a constant, or . . . as a variable that may shift from age to age? Is its content given us by deduction from unalterable premises, or by a toilsome process of induction from circumstances of time and place?

BENJAMIN CARDOZO

The fact is that freedom from government can only be sensibly considered as part of man's total freedom, which also includes freedom from non-governmental human pressures and freedom from inanimate circumstances which may require governmental help. For most of us, individual liberty for ourselves means governmental restriction on somebody else. If I am to enjoy a stretch of Maine seaside unbothered by trespassing picnickers, the law officers must exclude the picnickers from my property. My freedom is enhanced, theirs curtailed. Devotion to individualism for one's self is often, perhaps generally, coupled with a desire to restrict that of somebody else.

A. E. SUTHERLAND, JR.

*W*HEN Jesus enjoined his followers to render unto Caesar what was Caesar's due, he posed the most difficult problem of government. Where is the line between individual liberty and public authority? When does freedom become anarchy; and order stagnation? This ancient issue, particularly in its economic aspects, has been a major thread in the fabric of American history. An early manifestation was the struggle between the Hamiltonians and the Jeffersonians—which indicated that victory went to the side that could obtain judicial support. More accurately, a growing faith in democracy insured the supremacy of political power unless the judiciary intervened. The proliferation of industry following the Civil War posed the old conflict in new terms. Rapid industrialization provoked pressures which in due time brought legislation and then litigation. The Granger movement illustrates the problem. Prosperity incidental to war and momentous railroad expansion was followed in the seventies by agonizing agricultural depression. Having greeted the railroads generously, farmers soon discovered that freight rates were often discriminatory, if not extortionate. Competition, which had been relied upon as a regulator, was all but nonexistent. For relief the agrarians turned to their state legislatures and got the famous Granger legislation. This "hay-seed socialism" raised a classic issue: how far may the community interfere with private property in the interest of public well-being? Specifically, could a state regulate rates charged by privately owned railroads and grain elevators? To Chief Justice Waite and his Court this seemed hardly a legal issue. "We know that this [political power to regulate] may be abused; but that is no argument against its existence. For protection against abuses by legislatures the people must resort to the polls, not to the courts."[1] Having satisfied itself that authority to regulate was reserved to the states, the Court had exhausted its authority. Policy, i.e., the manner in which an acknowledged power is exercised, was deemed a matter for the political processes.

But the tide was soon running the other way. First by dicta, and then by decision,[2] the Granger cases along with judicial humility were abandoned. Justice Holmes, of the Massachusetts bench, suspected that fear of socialism

> [had] led people who no longer hope to control the legislatures to look to the courts as expounders of the Constitution, and that in some courts new principles have been discovered outside the bodies of those instruments, which may be generalized into acceptance of the economic doctrines [laissez faire] which prevailed about fifty years ago, and a wholesale prohibition of what a tribunal of lawyers does not think about right.[3]

In any case, before the end of the last century "laissez-faire" economics became constitutional law. In 1908 President Hadley, of Yale University, described the Court's new role:

> . . . the fundamental division of powers in the Constitution of the United States is between the voters on the one hand and the property owners on the other. The forces of democracy on the one side, divided between the executive and the legislature, are set over against the forces of property on the other side with the judiciary as arbiter between them.[4]

Mr. Justice Holmes's dissenting struggle against this judicial role may be summarized in what he wrote when the Court struck down New York's effort to provide a ten-hour workday for bakers:

> This case is decided upon an economic theory which a large part of the country does not entertain. If it were a question whether I agree with that theory, I should desire to study it further and long before making up my mind. But I do not conceive that to be my duty, because I strongly believe that my agreement or disagreement has nothing to do with the right of a majority to embody their opinion in law. . . .
> . . . I think that the word liberty in the Fourteenth Amendment is perverted when it is held to prevent the natural outcome of a dominant opinion, unless it can be said that a rational and fair man necessarily would admit that the statute proposed would infringe fundamental principles as they have been understood by the traditions of our people and our law.[5]

As Attorney General (later Mr. Justice) Jackson put it: "By 1933 the Court was no longer regarded as one of three equal departments among which the powers of government were distributed. Instead [it was said to be] 'invested with acknowledged and *supreme* authority,' and the whole conservative and property philosophy became oriented around 'judicial supremacy.' "[6]

Whatever may be said about discord within the new Court, on one issue there has been complete agreement: economic "laissez faire" is not basic law. By constitutionalizing it the old judges had transgressed upon the political processes. They had deprived the people of freedom to choose between competing economic policies. But how was the new Court to extricate itself? What is the true nature of the judicial function?

Mr. Justice Black's response starts with a series of "absolutes," which, if adopted by the Court, would radically alter the meaning of the First and Fourteenth amendments as well as the Commerce Clause on which some of his predecessors had been so vulnerable. Most business is conducted by corporations. To insure the states broad latitude in the regulation of economic affairs, the Justice insists that corporations should not be treated as "persons" within the protection of the Fourteenth Amendment.[7] To the same end he would drain all economic content out of Due Process and related generalities of the same amendment. What then shall they mean? Here the Justice looks for guidance to the Bill of Rights (which gives protection only against the national government). In sum, the Fourteenth Amendment (applying only to the states) should be read to give the same protection against state action which the Bill of Rights gives against national action.[8]

Further to free state power in economic affairs the Justice insists that the national power to regulate interstate commerce should have no force as a restraint upon the states. Here, however, he reluctantly relents in case of "patent" discrimination by a state against interstate trade.[9] But as a grant of power for congressional regulation of the economy, the Commerce Clause apparently would be as extensive as imagination might conceive. For congressional misuse, the remedy would be the polls; for abuse by the states (except as noted in the case of discrimination) the appeal would be to Congress. Allowing this full measure of economic control to the political processes, Mr. Justice Black would take special pains to insure their freedom. Thus First Amendment liberties—speech, press, religion, and assembly—would have a "preferred" constitutional status. State or national action touching upon them would lose the customary presumption of validity. Indeed, the presumption seems to be reversed:

Choice on that border [between individual freedom and public authority], now as always delicate, is perhaps more so where the usual presumption supporting legislation is balanced by the preferred place given in our scheme to the great, the indispensable democratic freedoms secured by the First Amendment. . . . That priority gives these liberties a sanctity and a sanction not permitting dubious intrusions. . . .

For these reasons any attempt to restrict those liberties must be justified by clear public interest, threatened not doubtfully or remotely, but by clear and present danger. The rational [man] connection between the remedy provided and the evil to be curbed, which in other contexts might support legislation against attack . . . will not suffice. These rights rest on firmer foundation. Accordingly whatever occasion would sustain orderly discussion and persuasion, at appropriate time and place, must have clear support in public danger, actual or impending. Only the gravest abuses, endangering paramount interests, give occasion for permissible limitation.[10]

Yet, concurring in this language, the Justice seems personally to go further:

I have always believed that the First Amendment is the keystone of our Government, that the freedoms it guarantees provide the best insurance against destruction of all freedom. At least as to speech in the realm of public matters, I believe that the "clear and present danger" test does not "mark the furthermost boundaries of protected expression" but does "no more than recognize a minimum compulsion of the Bill of Rights."[11]

Here is a clue to Mr. Justice Black's handling of the clear and present danger test. With one possible exception,[12] he has yet to find its standard satisfied. Whatever linguistic concessions he may make to his colleagues, his practice suggests that for him freedom of utterance on public affairs is virtually unlimited. Here are judicial views to match the democratic dream. Let the minds and souls of men be free, and self-government may be trusted to care for itself. How can men choose between good and bad, how can they know what is right or wrong, unless they are free to hear everything that may be said on all sides of every issue?

Between the old Court's conservative idealism and his brother Black's liberal idealism, Mr. Justice Frankfurter, as judge,
cannot distinguish. In his pragmatic view, ultimates—whether
economic or libertarian—are not for judges. He sees the Constitution as largely open-ended. Its essence is not an embodi-
ment of final substantive truths but an allocation of powers and
processes. Let the community by these *devices* choose its own
ends. Of course, the Constitution sets some limits. But it was
made "for people of fundamentally differing views" and for a
vast, unknowable future.

> From generation to generation fresh vindication is given to the
> prophetic wisdom of the framers of the Constitution in casting
> it in terms so broad that it has adaptable vitality for the drastic
> changes in our society which they knew to be inevitable, even
> though they could not foresee them. . . . The Constitution can-
> not be applied in disregard of the external circumstances in
> which men live and move and have their being.[13]

Its provisions cannot be treated by judges as "mathematical
abstractions." It has survived because its ample generality has
been able to accommodate differing value systems to meet a
progressive people's changing needs. Such meaning as it has
had is essentially the meaning given it in application. But
courts, as Mr. Justice Frankfurter sees it, are not the only
agencies of government that must breathe life into old parchment. Indeed, because their life-giving "interpretations" are
not subject to the restraints of political responsibility, they
are constantly at loggerheads with the basic principle of democratic government. Still the judicial "right [duty?] to pass
on validity of legislation is now too much part of our constitutional system to be brought into question."[14] And so, because
this function is "inherently oligarchic," in the "day to day
working of our democracy it is vital that [this] power of the
non-democratic organ of our Government be exercised with rig-
orous self-restraint."[15] But if restraint, i.e., objectivity, is crucial, no one is more conscious of the difficulty of capturing that
will-of-the-wisp than Mr. Justice Frankfurter—or of the vast

room for subjectivity which the flexible Constitution permits. Thus, to honor the accepted power of judicial review and avoid its tendency to degenerate into judicial supremacy, the Justice resorts to the ancient common-law device whereby jury findings are safeguarded from intrusion by judges. A statute, like a jury verdict, must stand regardless of how mistaken it may seem to judges, unless they are prepared to hold that reasonable men could not have found as the legislature (or jury) did find.

> It can never be emphasized too much that one's own opinion about the wisdom or evil of a law should be excluded altogether when one is doing one's duty on the bench. The only opinion of our own even looking in that direction that is material is our opinion whether legislators could in reason have enacted such a law. . . . I know of no other test which this Court is authorized to apply in nullifying legislation.[16]

Perhaps the Justice sees that just as it is a function of juries to temper the law with justice as understood by the community, so it is a function of legislatures to temper similarly the linguistic absolutes of the Constitution—at least when they collide with one another.[17] But fundamentally his position is founded upon a deep respect for popular self-government. The "reasonable man" test thus serves constitutional law as it served the common law, to allow some room for legal growth and yet preclude capricious, *ad hoc* adjudication. It does not give automatic answers. It will not make a great judge of a little man, and, like other tools, is subject to misuse. But at its best it does suggest an external standard for the guidance of a hard-pressed court; a standard rooted in what Holmes called the only sound basis for any legal system—"the actual feelings and demands of the community, whether right or wrong."

> Even where the social undesirability of a law may be convincingly urged, invalidation of the law by a court debilitates popular democratic government. Most laws dealing with economic and social problems are matters of trial and error. That which before trial appears to be demonstrably bad may belie prophecy in actual operation. It may not prove good, but it

may prove innocuous. But even if a law is found wanting on trial, it is better that its defects should be demonstrated and removed than that the law should be aborted by judicial fiat. Such an assertion of judicial power deflects responsibility from those on whom in a democratic society it ultimately rests—the people. . . .

But there is reason for judicial restraint in matters of policy deeper than the value of experiment: it is founded on a recognition of the gulf of difference between sustaining and nullifying legislation. . . . The Court is not saved from being oligarchic because it professes to act in the service of humane ends. As history amply proves, the judiciary is prone to misconceive the public good by confounding private notions with constitutional requirements, and such misconceptions are not subject to legitimate displacement by the will of the people except at too slow a pace. Judges appointed for life whose decisions run counter to prevailing opinion cannot be voted out of office and supplanted by men of views more consonant with it. They are even farther removed from democratic pressures by the fact that their deliberations are in secret and remain beyond disclosure either by periodic reports or by such a modern device for securing responsibility to the electorate as the "press conference." But a democracy need not rely on the courts to save it from its own unwisdom. If it is alert— and without alertness by the people there can be no enduring democracy—unwise or unfair legislation can readily be removed from the statute books. It is by such vigilance over its representatives that democracy proves itself.[18]

For Mr. Justice Frankfurter the judge's duty of humility applies with respect to all provisions of the Constitution, not just to those which one set of values or another may relegate to a deferred position.

The Constitution does not give us greater veto power when dealing with one phase of "liberty" than with another. . . . Judicial self-restraint is equally necessary whenever an exercise of political or legislative power is challenged. . . . Our power does not vary according to the particular provision of the Bill of Rights which is invoked. The right not to have property taken without just compensation has, so far as the scope of judicial power is concerned, the same constitutional dignity as the right to be protected against unreasonable searches and seizures, and the latter has no less claim than freedom of the press or freedom of speech or religious freedom. . . . [R]esponsibility for legislation lies with legislatures, answerable as they are directly to the people, and this Court's only and very narrow function is to determine whether within the broad grant of authority vested in legislatures they have exercised a judgment for which reasonable justification can be offered.[19]

Of course where the Constitution speaks clearly there is no problem. The constant difficulty is that for many purposes its meaning and application are questionable. This indeed is its genius. To resolve their own doubts and disagreements, to accommodate an unknowable future, the Founding Fathers (like the amenders) generally used undefined terms of calculated vagueness. Each generation's birthright then is to find its own wisdom—or the opposite—in the ancient document. And so the Constitution lives despite unforeseen vicissitudes because it derives vitality from the life about it. That is why Mr. Justice Brandeis stressed so heavily the factual setting in which constitutional issues arise.

Wise and devoted democrats believe that we threaten freedom when we send Communist leaders to jail as in the *Dennis* case.[20] Equally wise and devoted democrats believe that we jeopardize freedom unduly if we do not send them to jail. Neither position, one suggests, is demonstrably true or false, or unequivocally written in the Constitution. Shall the choice be made by the judicial or the political processes? By the few or by the many?[21] Despite broad language in the First Amendment, no judge and no responsible commentator has argued that it embraces every spoken word regardless of circumstances.[22] As with the "rights of property," the question always has been how and where to locate appropriate boundaries. We may call this "interpretation," if we choose, but surely in the absence of express constitutional limitations it is largely a law-creating process—and not less so in the hands of liberals than in the hands of conservatives.[23]

Accordingly, for Mr. Frankfurter the substitution of judicial judgment for the judgment of those to whom primary governmental responsibility has been given can never be justified by amorphous proprietarian or libertarian generalities. If the Constitution is to be a living instrument of government, the breath of life must come from the community—not from a few "independent" judges. It follows that judicial interference with the extra judicial processes of government is permissible only when the concrete facts of a specific case leave no room for doubt, i.e., when the Court is prepared to hold that no reasonable mind could support the challenged legislative view. *This is to say simply that uncertainty is to be resolved in favor of the wisdom and integrity of sister organs of government and the people to whom they are responsible.* For doubt entails choice, and choice in a democracy belongs to the political processes.

Judicial idealists—both the "laissez-faire" and the libertarian variety—accept this approach as orthodox in all cases not involving their respective "preferred place" interests. The exception for "property rights" in the one case, and for "personal liberty" in the other, inevitably turns on the alleged fundamental nature of the favored interest. But even if we could agree on what claims are to have preference, there would still be a cruel dilemma. How can democracy work if its fundamentals are not preserved? Yet how can democracy prosper, how great is our respect for it, if we do not trust it with fundamentals? What is left of it if we are not prepared to honor even those fruits of the democratic process which are not beyond support by reasonable men, i.e., not plainly outlawed by generally accepted legal norms?

FREEDOM OF EXPRESSION AND ASSOCIATION

A basic weakness of dictatorship is that it relies upon the thinking power of a chosen few. Minds outside the inner circle are drugged into submissive stupor—or eliminated—by all the arts that modern psychology can muster. It is like running an automobile on less than all its cylinders. That, perhaps, is why dictatorships are relatively unstable and short-lived. The genius of democracy is its willingness to garner wisdom from the total brain-power of the community. Uncommunicated ideas serve no social, and little, if any, private purpose. Without freedom to communicate there is small incentive or stimulation for thought. The most subtle of punishments is solitary confinement. The imprisoned mind decays. For these reasons freedom of speech, press, and assembly are the foundations of democracy, the tools of society's thinking process.

Democracy, then, is the *unfettered exchange of ideas* with public control of *action* in accordance with those thoughts which win acceptance in the market place of reason. The great difficulty, as Learned Hand has observed, is that words may be used not only as "keys of discussion" but as "triggers" of harmful action.[24] Because the ideal of democracy is government by reason, the free interchange of ideas is given special constitutional protection by the First and Fourteenth amendments. Yet words in certain contexts may threaten *action* which the community has had no opportunity to discuss and accept or reject. This belies government by consent of the governed. Falsely crying fire in a dark and crowded theater is not calculated to start a rational discussion. Such "force-words" are not part of society's thinking process. Thus they are not entitled to the very special protection which the Bill of Rights gives to "discussion-words." Shouting fire in a theater is at one extreme; a graduate seminar is at the other. Such cases present no great problems. But how shall the line be drawn in the penumbra between the extremes where "thought merges into action"? The difficulty is often magnified by an irritated climate of opinion as in the cold war vis-à-vis the problem of subversion.

In *Dennis* v. *United States* the accused were charged with conspiracy to organize the American Communist Party and "to advocate and teach" the violent overthrow of government. They challenged the Smith Act, on which the charge was based, as a restraint upon free speech. The Supreme Court ruled against them. Mr. Justice Black, dissenting, argued that the offending discourse was "in the realm of public matters." Thus with respect to it, the clear and present danger rule marks only "the minimum compulsion of the Bill of Rights." Even the judges who upheld conviction recognized that the conduct in issue had posed no present danger. Accordingly, Mr. Justice Black insisted, the Communists could not be punished:

> Here again . . . my basic disagreement with the Court is not as to how we should explain or reconcile what was said in prior decisions but springs from a fundamental difference in constitutional approach. . . . At the outset I want to emphasize what the crime involved in this case is, and what it is not. These [parties] were not charged with an attempt to over-throw the Government. They were not charged with overt acts of any kind designed to overthrow the Government. The charge was that they agreed to assemble and to talk and publish certain ideas at a later date: The indictment is that they conspired to organize the Communist Party and to use speech or newspapers and other publications in the future to teach and advocate the forceable overthrow of the Government. No matter how it is worded, this is a virulent form of prior censorship of speech and press, which I believe the First Amendment forbids. . . .
>
> Public opinion being what it now is, few will protest the conviction of these Communist petitioners. There is hope, however, that in calmer times . . . this or some later Court will restore the First Amendment liberties to the high preferred place where they belong in a free society.[25]

Mr. Justice Frankfurter concurred with the majority. He could not treat discourse as monolithic and fungible. Some utterances have far greater claim to protection than others:

> Not every type of speech occupies the same position on the scale of values. There is no substantial public interest in permitting . . . "the lewd and obscene, the profane, the libelous, and the insulting or 'fighting' words—those which by their very utterance inflict injury or tend to incite an immediate breach of the peace." . . . We have frequently indicated that the interest in protecting speech depends on the circumstances of the occasion. It is pertinent to the decision before us to consider where on

the scale of values we have in the past placed the type of speech now claiming constitutional immunity·

Then, finding that conspiratorial teaching and advocacy of violence "ranks low" . . . "[o]n any scale of values which we have hitherto recognized," the Justice considered the interests which Congress had found at stake on the other side of the scale— national self-preservation vis-à-vis the Communist menace. On balance he could not say that Congress in the Smith Act had gone beyond the realm of reason. Thus in his view to inquire further would be an intrusion into the legislative domain.

For those who find in this position a retreat from the Justice's lifelong, off-the-bench liberalism, it should be noted that years before he left Harvard he wrote,

> It must never be forgotten that our constant preoccupation with the constitutionality of legislation rather than its wisdom tends to preoccupation of the American mind with a false value. Even the most rampant worshiper of judicial supremacy admits that wisdom and justice are not the tests of constitutionality. Even the extreme right of the [old] Supreme Court occasionally sustain laws which they abominate. But the tendency of focusing attention on constitutionality is to make constitutionality synonymous with propriety; to regard a law as all right so long as it is "constitutional." Such an attitude is a great enemy of liberalism. Particularly in legislation affecting freedom of thought and freedom of speech *much that is highly illiberal would be clearly constitutional.* . . . [T]he real battles of liberalism are not won in the Supreme Court. To a large extent the Supreme Court . . . is the reflector of that impalpable but controlling thing, the general drift of public opinion. Only a persistent, positive translation of the liberal faith into the thoughts and acts of the community is the real reliance against the unabated temptation to strait-jacket the human mind.[26]

Difficulty increases when contending claims are more evenly matched than they were in the *Dennis* case. Freedom of the press is a basic constitutional principle and so is a fair trial. What is the Court to do when such crucial interests collide, as when newspaper editorials put pressure upon a trial court in pending litigation? Potent arguments may be made on both sides, but surely the Constitution does not clearly proclaim an answer. Yet one must be found. If general propositions are to be decisive, which shall it be—FREE SPEECH or FAIR TRIAL? Is the intensity of a judge's feeling for one or the other to be decisive? Such were the difficulties presented in *Times-Mirror v. Superior Court of California*.[27] Mr. Justice Black, speaking for the Court, did not openly assert that a free press is more important than a free judiciary. Yet he made that appraisal implicitly by resorting to the clear and present danger test— whose avowed new purpose is to give utterance a preferred status. Having chosen his legal ground, he then *reappraised* the evidence and found no imminent danger. Indeed, he went further and found that the state trial and supreme courts were even wrong in finding that the editorials had a "reasonable tendency" toward harm.

Mr. Justice Frankfurter dissented. Finding no clear answer in the Constitution, he did not pretend that one was there. The power of courts to protect the administration of justice from outside pressures is an old tradition. Even First Amendment freedoms depend in part upon protection by fair trials. And so, finding no special circumstances to remove all doubt, the Justice would not override a state's decision to give priority to the trial (or, presumably, to the press). In this view different jurisdictions would be free to try different solutions for the curse of "trial by newspaper." Experience so gained would provide grist for the lawmaking process. Such is the implication of Holmes's teaching that the life of the law is not logic but experience.

Are there cases in which Mr. Justice Frankfurter is prepared to override a legislative choice of values? In *Sweezy* v. *New Hampshire* a state un-American activities "committee" had questioned the accused about the Progressive Party. He testified that he knew of no Communist connection therewith and refused to answer further on the ground that the questions "infringed upon the inviolability of the right to privacy in his political thoughts, actions and associations." In a concurring opinion Mr. Justice Frankfurter found merit in these claims:

> For a citizen to be made to forego even a part of so basic a liberty as his political autonomy, the subordinating interest of the State must be compelling. . . . [The] inviolability of privacy belonging to a citizen's political loyalties has so overwhelming an importance to the well-being of our kind of society that it cannot be constitutionally encroached upon on the basis of so meagre a countervailing interest of the State as may be argumentatively found in the remote, shadowy threat to the security of New Hampshire allegedly presented in the origins and contributing elements of the Progressive Party and in petitioner's relations to these. . . . Whatever, on the basis of massive proof and in the light of history, of which this Court may well take judicial notice, be the justification for not regarding the Communist Party as a conventional political party, no such justification has been afforded in regard to the Progressive Party. A foundation in fact and reason would have to be established far weightier than the intimations that appear in the record to warrant such a view of the Progressive Party. . . .
>
> To be sure, this is a conclusion based on a judicial judgment in balancing two contending principles—the right of a citizen to political privacy, as protected by the Fourteenth Amendment, and the right of the State to self protection. And striking the balance implies the exercise of judgment. This is the inescapable judicial task in giving substantive content, legally enforced, to the Due Process Clause, and it is a task ultimately committed to this Court. It must not be an exercise of whim or will. It must be an overriding judgment founded on something much deeper and more justifiable than personal preference. As far as it lies within human limitations, it must be an impersonal judgment. It must rest on fundamental presuppositions rooted in history to which widespread acceptance may fairly be attributed. Such a judgment must be arrived at in a spirit of humility when it counters the judgment of the State's highest court. But, in the end, judgment cannot be escaped—the judgment of this Court.[28]

Characteristically, the Justice does not pretend that his conclusion is literally prescribed in the Constitution. He rests rather on "fundamental presuppositions rooted in history to which widespread acceptance may fairly be attributed." These for him elucidate the written words. Or as he put it in the *Sweezy* case, "While the language of the Constitution does not change, the changing circumstances of a progressive society for which it was designed yield new and fuller import to its meaning." No doubt this would have pleased Thomas Reed Powell, who in his final summation observed that what he "most objected to in many judges is something that springs from a feeling of judicial duty to try to make out that their conclusions come from the Constitution."[29]

Dennis, perhaps, may be classified as a case in which a relatively weak private interest collided with a major public interest. Such at least was the legislative appraisal, and Mr. Justice Frankfurter could not find it so unreasonable as to warrant a judicial veto. In *Sweezy*, at the other extreme, the Justice found a formidable private, vis-à-vis an amorphous public, interest. The discrepancy seemed so gross that he could not find a contrary legislative appraisal within the bounds of reason. And so with unveiled misgiving he voted, as he seldom does in such cases, against the state's position. The *Times-Mirror* case perhaps falls somewhere between these two extremes. There the Justice found the contesting claims—fair trial versus free press—so evenly balanced as to preclude judicial intrusion upon state policy.

No doubt such judicial balancing of interests (more accurately, such sitting in judgment upon balances struck by others) is dangerous business. Yet it is inevitable on Mr. Justice Frankfurter's premise that judicial review is a historic duty, though the written Constitution rarely gives clear answers for hard cases. Some insist that regardless of what a judge may profess, he cannot long escape his own sense of justice, i.e., his own bias. Objectivity may belong to the gods—or to demons. "Be that as it may," says Learned Hand, "we know that men do differ widely in this capacity; and the incredulity which seeks to discredit that knowledge is a part of the crusade against reason from which we have already so bitterly suffered. We may deny—and, if we are competent observers, we will deny—that no one can be aware of the danger [of his bias] and in large measure provide against it."[30] Judge Hand's career on the bench, like those of Holmes, Brandeis, Stone, and Cardozo, are monuments to the truth of this insight.

Mr. Justice Black cannot accept the second part of his colleague's premise. To him the Constitution speaks clearly, at least with respect to utterance on public affairs. The First Amendment forbids laws "abridging the freedom of speech, or of the press. . . ." There are no explicit qualifications. Nor is this a matter of passing interest. As the Justice sees it, "Freedom to speak and write about public questions is as important to the life of our government as is the heart to the human body. . . . If that heart be weakened, the result is debilitation; if it be stilled, the result is death."[31] The verbal clarity of the Constitution and the importance of the interests concerned are Mr. Justice Black's shield against critics who charge him with ignoring the special facts of each particular case. Those to whom the old document speaks less clearly cannot otherwise explain how he "always" reaches the same result regardless of the circumstances involved. As Mr. Justice Jackson charged in the *Terminiello* case,[32] the libertarians

> [reverse] this conviction by reiterating generalized approbations of freedom of speech with which, in the abstract, no one will disagree. Doubts as to their applicability are lulled by avoidance of more than passing reference to the circumstances of Terminiello's speech and judging it as if he had spoken to persons as dispassionate as empty benches, or like a modern Demosthenes practicing his Philippics on a lonely seashore.

The background of this case is worth attention. Terminiello, a suspended priest, spoke in a Chicago auditorium to about eight hundred persons under the sponsorship of the Christian Veterans of America. His speech, according to Mr. Justice Jackson (just back from the Nürnberg Trials), "followed, with fidelity that is more than coincidental, the pattern of European fascist leaders." Linking Democrats, Jews, and Communists together as common "conspirators," it was rife with racial hatred. Outside, a hostile crowd (Communist-led, according to Terminiello) milled about, yelling and throwing stones. Police were unable to prevent violence including some smashing of doors and windows. Mr. Justice Jackson saw in this episode a struggle between "totalitarian groups" for what Hitler called "the conquest of the streets" as the "key to power in the state." Is this the free discussion, the tool of democracy, which the First Amendment's unqualified language was meant to protect?

Often where Mr. Justice Black sees one great and overriding value, others find competing claims not without constitutional sanction—as in *Dennis* and *Times-Mirror* as well as *Terminiello*. Carl Swisher claims that "the eloquent defenses of civil liberty . . . written . . . by Justices Black and Douglas, take much of their drive from the fact that the dynamics of opposing [interests] are largely ignored."[33] The answer no doubt would be that opposing interests are not ignored but seen in true perspective.

It is not wholly accurate to suggest that Mr. Justice Black *always* discounts every consideration that might limit utterance. He spoke for the Court in *Gibony* v. *Empire Storage & Ice Co.*[34] This involved an injunction against picketing designed to compel the company to violate a state antitrust law. The Justice upheld the injunction, though he insists that picketing is a modern form of free speech:

> The [state] policy against restraints of trade is of long standing. . . . It is clearly drawn in an attempt to afford all persons an equal opportunity to buy goods. There was clear danger, imminent and immediate, that unless restrained, [the picketers] would succeed in making that policy a dead letter. . . . [Their] power with that of their allies was irresistible. And it is clear that [they] were doing more than exercising a right of free speech or press.

Here was a clash between a "preferred" and a more mundane interest in which Mr. Justice Black upheld a state's choice in favor of the mundane. The decisive element, of course, was that here he found the picketers had engaged in "more than" mere discourse. No doubt; but was nothing more than discourse involved in the *Dennis* case? More, that is, which Congress, judge and jury were entitled to consider? Of course the conspiracy charged was not conspiracy to overthrow government but only to teach and advocate the doctrine of overthrow. As Mr. Justice Douglas emphasized, it would be wrong to confuse the two. Acknowledging this, Mr. Justice Frankfurter observed that "it would be equally wrong to treat [defendants' conduct] as a seminar in political theory." Here, as in the cases of *Terminiello*, *Times-Mirror*, and *Gibony*, he found a hybrid problem that entailed more than mere expression of ideas, yet less than forthright, illegal action. If only open discussion is involved there is no great problem; nor is there when nothing but overt action is in issue. For most judges the quandary in these cases is that they contain some elements of both and often more besides. What Learned Hand said of Mr. Justice Cardozo seems relevant here: "He never disguised the difficulties. . . ."[35] Or as Frankfurter put it with respect to Hand: ". . . he does not meet difficulties by evading them. Intricate problems do not appear simple to him, nor does he make them appear simple to others by verbal legerdemain."[36]

FREEDOM OF RELIGION

Only after providing for the claims of the soul did the Founders turn to political liberty. The first freedom singled out for protection in the Bill of Rights was freedom of religion. This is a dual concept. There shall be no law "respecting an establishment of religion," and none "prohibiting the free exercise thereof." Does the former require a complete separation of church and state? Or does it mean simply that government shall not give preferences to this or that religious belief (leaving it free to give impartial aid and solace)? The riddle of "free exercise" is more complex. Sincere religious practice often clashes with crucial secular powers of government as, for example, the power to raise and train an army, or even to levy taxes. "Religion" is not a term of precise content. What it means to some is often highly offensive to others. Because there is such a variety of religious belief, things spiritual and political impinge upon each other endlessly. The rub is that free exercise "embraces two concepts—freedom to believe and freedom to act. The first," the Court has said, "is absolute but, in the nature of things, the second cannot be."[37] Again the judge's problem is how and where to draw a line. And here again pragmatism and idealism are apt to have quite different thrusts.

In *Martin* v. *Struthers*,[38] Mr. Justice Black held for the Court that a city may not hinder distribution of religious handbills by forbidding uninvited door-to-door solicitation. Mr. Justice Frankfurter rejected the implication that the Constitution outlaws impartial efforts to protect the privacy of the home from uninvited intrusion. Particularly did that privacy seem important in Struthers, a small industrial community most of whose residents worked in steel plants, then operating on an around-the-clock, wartime schedule. Thus for some

> portions of the city's inhabitants, opportunities for sleep and refreshment require during the day as well as night whatever peace and quiet is attainable in a modern industrial town. It is further recognized that the modern multiple residences give opportunities for pseudo-canvassers to ply evil trades—dangers to the community pursued by the few but far-reaching in their success and in the fears they arouse.

Even the libertarian Zachariah Chafee had pointed out,

> Of all the methods of spreading unpopular ideas, [house-to-house canvassing] seems the least entitled to extensive protection. The possibilities of persuasion are slight compared with the certainties of annoyance. Great as is the value of exposing citizens to novel views, home is one place where a man ought to be able to shut himself up in his own ideas if he desires. There he should be free not only from unreasonable searches and seizures but also from hearing uninvited strangers expound distasteful doctrines. A doorbell cannot be disregarded like a handbill.[39]

These views and those of Mr. Justice Frankfurter seem at least partially to have prevailed—over a Black dissent—in *Breard* v. *Alexandria*.[40]

Struthers, perhaps, may be an extreme case in the sense that *Dennis* was extreme. In each, as legislative authority saw it, an extravagant claim of aggressive individual right collided with a relatively more important community interest. A closer balance of contending forces, comparable to that in the *Times-Mirror* case, may be involved when religious conscience takes offense at a required flag salute in public schools. Again Mr. Justice Black and the Court rejected a state's legislative evaluation of the clashing claims.[41] The community had sought to "promote respect for the flag and for this country" as part of its educational program. The objection was that this compelled a bowing down to graven images in violation of religious belief. But in the Court's view:

> Neither our domestic tranquility in peace nor our martial effort in war depends on compelling little children to participate in a ceremony which ends in nothing for them but a fear of spiritual condemnation. If, as we think, their fears are groundless, time and reason are the proper antidotes for their errors.

Mr. Justice Frankfurter could not believe that courts have any marked competence for appraising such subtle interests. Judges specialize in law, not religious and educational values. We "should be very diffident in setting [our] judgment against that of a state in determining what is and what is not a major concern, what means are appropriate to proper ends, and what is the total social cost in striking the balance of imponderables." In short, here again Mr. Justice Frankfurter found conflict of basic interests in a context not so plain as to justify a judge in holding the legislative choice erroneous beyond all reasonable doubt:

> The essence of religious freedom guaranteed by our Constitution is . . . this: no religion shall either receive the state's support or incur its hostility. Religion is outside the sphere of political government. This does not mean that all matters on

which religious organizations or beliefs may pronounce are outside the sphere of government. Were this so, instead of the separation of church and state, there would be the subordination of the state on any matter deemed within the sovereignty of the religious conscience. Much that is the concern of temporal authority affects the spiritual interests of men. But it is not enough to strike down a non-discriminatory law that it may hurt or offend some dissident view.

When such vital interests collide and reasonable minds may disagree as to what priority the Constitution gives, accommodations must be made. The "real question is, who is to make such accommodations, the courts or the legislature?"

If the door-to-door solicitation case presents one extreme imbalance of contentions, the "released time" cases seem to present the other. In *Zorach* v. *Clauson*[42] public school students were "released" to permit attendance at sectarian classes of their own choosing outside the public schools. No student was compelled to take religious instruction, but all students had either to take it or stay in school. Unexcused failure to attend one or the other was punishable under compulsory school attendance laws. Both Justices Black and Frankfurter dissented from the Court's "approval" of this system. As the former put it:

> Here the sole question is whether New York can use its compulsory education laws to help religious sects get attendants presumably too unenthusiastic to go unless moved to do so by the pressure of this state machinery. That this is the plan, purpose, design and consequence of the New York program cannot be denied. . . . In considering whether a state has entered this forbidden field the question is not whether it has entered too far but whether it has entered at all. New York is manipulating its compulsory education laws to help religious sects get pupils. This is not separation but combination of Church and State.

Mr. Justice Frankfurter was guided here, if not by terms of crystal clarity in the Constitution, by a then recent, all-but-unanimous decision in *Illinois ex rel. McCollum* v. *Board of*

Education.[43] This both he and Mr. Justice Black found indistinguishable from the New York case.

Perhaps the oldest element in the Anglo-American dream of freedom is one that first found expression in Magna Charta. The king shall not proceed against his subjects except by "the law of the land." Or, in the more modern terminology of the Fourteenth Amendment, "No State . . . shall deprive any person of life, liberty, or property without due process of law." Linguistically and historically this is a procedural admonition. Its basic aim was to guarantee fair trials. Obviously such a concept cannot be captured in a neat, catchall rule of thumb. Still, Judge Learned Hand seems to have caught its essence when he said that it embodies the English sporting sense of fair play. Surely this at best is broad, even when confined to procedural problems. Yet, beginning in the 1890's, the old "laissez-faire" Court stretched it even wider to protect substantive economic interests. It became in sum a judicial weapon to strike down social legislation, as in the New York bakers' case.[44]

Mr. Justice Holmes observed that only the sky was the limit to what the old Court might do in the name of Due Process to legislative policy. As we have seen, all of the new judges reject the raising of economic "laissez faire" to the status of a constitutional mandate. Perhaps Mr. Justice Black fears that what has been done may be done again. In any event he has a penchant for Doric simplicity in the meaning of the Constitution. Hence, as we have seen, his *Adamson* retreat into the eighteenth century to find in the Bill of Rights the meaning of a Civil War amendment. Specifically, his proposition was that the three generalities of the Fourteenth Amendment—Due Process, Privileges and Immunities, and Equal Protection— "separately, and as a whole," accomplish this result.

When abuse of Due Process by the old Court was at its zenith, Professor Frankfurter argued that "The due process clauses ought to go." As he saw it then, no nine men are good and wise enough to wield the vast power which the old regime had found within the vague contours of those provisions.[45] But they remain, and on the bench such private views are irrelevant.

> These are very broad terms by which to accommodate freedom and authority. As has been suggested from time to time, they may be too large to serve as the basis for adjudication, in that they allow much room for individual notions of policy. . . . The fact is that the duty of such adjudication on a basis no less narrow has been committed to this Court.[46]

It does not follow that personal notions are to fill in what Mr. Justice Holmes called the "void of 'due process.' " When substantive regulations of economic affairs are at issue, it is "immaterial that [they] may run counter to the economic wisdom either of Adam Smith or J. Maynard Keynes, or may be ultimately mischievous even from the point of view of avowed state policy. Our inquiry must be much narrower."[47] Namely, is the challenged measure such, to use Holmes's language, "that a rational and fair man necessarily would admit that the statute proposed would infringe fundamental principles as they have been understood by the traditions of our people and our law"?[48]

But the problem is different when Due Process in its procedural aspects is before the Court. Here, if anywhere, that term has meaning and the judiciary a historic responsibility— not to make policy, but to see that policy is fairly enforced.

> Procedural fairness, if not all that originally was meant by due process of law, is at least what it most uncompromisingly requires. Procedural due process is more elemental and less flexible than substantive due process. It yields less to the times, varies less with conditions, and defers much less to legislative judgment. Insofar as it is technical law, it must be a specialized responsibility within the competence of the judiciary on which they do not bend before political branches of Government, as they should on matters of policy which comprise substantive law.[49]

Brandeis had made the point when he said, "One can never be

sure of ends—political, social, economic. There must always be doubt and difference of opinion; one can be 51 per cent sure." But as to means there is not the same room for speculation. Here ". . . fundamentals do not change; centuries of thought have established standards."[50] Even so, as Mr. Justice Frankfurter points out, ". . . due process is not a mechanical instrument. It is not a yardstick. It is a process. It is a delicate process of adjustment inescapably involving the exercise of judgment by those whom the Constitution entrusted with the unfolding of the process."[51]

Obviously Justices Black and Frankfurter start on common ground in recognizing the vagueness of Due Process. But Mr. Justice Frankfurter, constantly preoccupied with the living quality of the Constitution, cannot find comfort in his colleague's withdrawal into the eighteenth century. He cannot accept the idea that the Anglo-American concept of a fair trial meant no more in 1868 when the Fourteenth Amendment was adopted than it meant in 1791 when the Bill of Rights became law. Nor can he accept the thought that what had been known and experienced in 1791, or even 1868, must be the end of the development of judicial fairness. Part of the Bill of Rights ". . . grew out of transient experience and formulated remedies which time might well improve. The Fourteenth Amendment did not mean to imprison the States into the limited experience of the eighteenth century."[52] Black's formula for doing so, moreover, gets nowhere: to find meaning in the Due Process clause of the Fourteenth Amendment he "incorporates" the equally vague Due Process clause of the Fifth Amendment. But the "short answer" to the suggestion that Due Process means what the Bill of Rights means is that this is a strange way of saying so.[53]

What then are Mr. Justice Frankfurter's guideposts? Nothing less than "those canons of decency and fairness which express the notions of justice of English-speaking peoples."[54] Essentially, what is involved is a "judgment that reflects deep, even if inarticulate, feelings of our society. Judges must divine that feeling as best they can from all the relevant evidence and light which they can bring to bear. . . ."; and then, parenthetically, "It is noteworthy that while American experience has been drawn upon in the framing of constitutions for other democratic countries, the Due Process clause has not been copied."[55] Here, too, personal views must not be allowed to color judgment.

> The nature of the duty . . . makes it especially important to be humble in exercising it. Humility in this context means an alert self-scrutiny so as to avoid infusing into the vagueness of a Constitutional command one's merely private notions. Like other mortals, judges, though unaware, may be in the grip of prepossessions. The only way to relax such a grip . . . is to explore the influences that have shaped one's unanalyzed views in order to lay bare prepossessions.[56]

There is another—a federalistic—dimension to the problem. Whatever its content the Fourteenth Amendment is a restraint upon states' rights—and states' *responsibilities*. The broader its content, the less that is left to local self-government *in local affairs*. The narrower its content, the narrower the federal shield for the individual. Obviously Justices Black and Frankfurter agree that Due Process is less informative than constitutional provisions ought to be. In seeking standards for guidance in its application they disagree as to where the balance should be struck between past and present; between states' rights and individual interests; between the role of the courts and the role of the people in giving content to the American dream of individual freedom and local self-government.

Mr. Justice Frankfurter's position on this issue is orthodox. Apart from the "laissez-faire" fiasco, it has been followed by the Court from the beginning. If Mr. Justice Black's attack is broad, the difference in the two views seems to center in practice on the "right to counsel." Must a state furnish lawyers for indigent defendants in criminal cases? This narrow, if important, point at which the main pinch comes illustrates again the basic differences in the conceptual and pragmatic approaches.

Mr. Justice Frankfurter (and the Court) would fire off the Due Process blunderbuss only upon a showing that an indigent defendant did, *in fact*, suffer for want of counsel. In short, the fair conduct of state trials is essentially a state responsibility—only for actual, demonstrated unfairness is federal interference justified.[57]

> At best . . . intervention by this Court in the criminal process of States is delicate business. It should not be indulged in unless no reasonable doubt is left that a State denies, or has refused to exercise, means of correcting a claimed infraction of the United States Constitution. Intervention by this Court in the administration of the criminal justice of a State has all the disadvantages of interference from without. Whatever short-cut to relief may be had in a particular case, it is calculated to beget misunderstanding and friction and to that extent detracts from those imponderables which are the ultimate reliance of a civilized system of law. After all, this is the Nation's ultimate judicial tribunal, not a super-legal-aid bureau.[58]

This coldly cerebral approach is not for Mr. Justice Black. His generous heart is ever responsive to those who excite sympathy. Dissenting, he would follow an iron rule that, regardless of any showing of fairness or unfairness, no state trial can be valid unless the accused has (or properly waives) aid of counsel.[59] But what of a Due Process case cursed with a modern form of unfairness not contemplated by the "specific" provisions of the eighteenth-century Bill of Rights? Such was the problem in *Griffin* v. *Illinois*.[60] To preserve the eyesight of its judges, Illinois requires that the record of a case on appeal be presented in printed form. But suppose a convict cannot pay the high cost of printing? Apart from the principle of Due Process, the Bill of Rights says not a word on the subject. Without explanation, Mr. Justice Black went along with his brother Frankfurter and the Court in seeing to it that Griffin had a fair hearing. So, too, the Bill of Rights does not explicitly outlaw convictions based on false evidence knowingly introduced; nor criminal statutes which do not adequately define what conduct is illegal; nor indeed racial discrimination. Yet in cases raising these problems, as in the *Griffin* case, Mr. Justice Black came out of the eighteenth century and silently accepted the orthodox view of Due Process (along with Equal Protection) as a dynamic, living concept.[61]

Just as the Justice sometimes finds more in the Fourteenth Amendment than his *Adamson* rule permits, so on occasion he may find less. The Bill of Rights provides for indictment by grand jury and for jury trials in *all* criminal cases and in civil cases involving more than twenty dollars.[62] It seems unlikely that, if put to the test, Mr. Justice Black would insist that these are fully imposed upon the states by the Fourteenth Amendment. Indictment by grand jury is a costly and cumbersome thing inspired by social conditions that no longer exist. Even when the Fourteenth Amendment was adopted almost half of the ratifying states had abandoned or qualified the old indictment system. Today more than half the states have done so. For minor offenses at the state and local level the petit jury has become all but obsolete. It is not to be forgotten that the right to jury trials in *all* federal prosecutions was adopted on the accurate assumption that there would be relatively few categories of federal crime and that generally what there were would be weighty. Thus to insist upon a right to trial by jury for *all* petty state and local offenses would be as great a perversion as to insist upon it in all state civil cases involving more than twenty dollars.[63] The significance of that sum was one thing in 1791; it is something very different today. Indeed, by act of Congress, federal trial courts ordinarily do not now have jurisdiction to hear civil cases involving less than ten thousand dollars.

Apart from these three provisions—which presumably even Mr. Justice Black would not fully "incorporate" despite his *Adamson* argument—the Court has not found in Due Process any less than was *originally contemplated* by the Bill of Rights. After all, the historic meaning of the Sixth Amendment "right to counsel" was the right to *employ*, not to have counsel furnished by government.[64] The Fourth Amendment presumably meant what it says in outlawing unreasonable search and seizure—but it says nothing about the exclusion from a trial of wholly reliable (if improperly obtained) evidence.[65] Freedom from double jeopardy, of course, was meant to bar harassment by repeated trials for the same offense. It is something very different to hold that government cannot appeal a case to correct errors so as to insure *one fair trial*.[66] Freedom from self-incrimination evidently was meant to outlaw Star Chamber tactics; to prevent a prosecutor from commenting to the jury upon failure of the accused to testify is another matter.[67]

Plainly, in federal prosecutions the Court goes beyond the historical meaning of the Bill of Rights. Refusal to impose the "new" meanings upon the states rests in part, of course, on federalistic considerations. It may also reflect a belief that some, at least, are no longer as wise and effective as they seemed in the era of "rugged individualism" from which they came. The federal rule that upsets convictions based on unquestionably true, if improperly obtained, evidence helps the guilty; it does nothing for the innocent whose privacy has been invaded illegally. More direct sanctions for protecting the innocent as well as the guilty are available to any state that wants them. To deny government a right of appeal in the interest of *one fair trial*, while allowing it to convicts, smacks of treating the public in the serious business of law enforcement on a heads-I-win, tails-you-lose basis. To deny prosecutors the power to comment on the accused's failure to testify seems unimportant. With or without such comment, men acting as jurors are not apt to reject the kind of inference that comes naturally in their everyday experience. Of course, all who stand accused of crime ought to have assistance of counsel. But (as the Department of Justice has told Congress repeatedly) the only effective way to get it for the impecunious is through legislative appropriations.

Meanwhile *Powell* v. *Alabama*[68] and *Betts* v. *Brady*[69] provide a federal remedy for those who can make a reasonable showing that, in fact, they suffered for want of counsel. To go farther with Mr. Justice Black would free convicts, who, well aware of their guilt, plead guilty, not wanting counsel (or jury) to prolong their agony. Of course a change of heart comes after time assuages the burden of guilt. Many such men by the efforts of prosecutors and trial judges had fair trials, though they were not represented by counsel. No doubt, too, there are others behind bars of whom this cannot be said—whether or not they had legal assistance. The full import of Mr. Justice Frankfurter's position in state right-to-counsel cases can be appreciated only when it is remembered that he is not to be outdone in strict enforcement of meticulous standards in *federal* criminal proceedings.[70] Clearly the Justice finds his *supervisory* duty with respect to the lower federal courts quite different from his constitutional function with respect to state judicial sysems. That he has a record second to none in safeguarding the procedural interests of those accused of federal crime need not be "explained" by a supposed special concern for the passive as against the aggressive liberties.[71] The deference due a *legislative* determination as to when the proselytizing interests of Communists, for example, must give way in the interest of national security is one thing; what is due a *police officer* who on his own undertakes to search without a warrant, or to obtain confessions by force, is something quite different. But what of a case in which the high deference due state proceedings is countered by the low deference due unauthorized police activities? Which consideration, for example, is to prevail on appeal from a state conviction based on the fruits of a policeman's unauthorized search? In *Wolf* v. *Colorado*,[72] Mr. Justice Frankfurter, writing for the Court, struck a balance somewhere between the two extremes. Characteristically, the balance struck was predicated not on the high standards which the Justice would doubtless require if he were acting as legislator or police chief but upon an objective, outside norm—the practice of a majority of state (indeed a majority of all Anglo-American supreme) courts. Surely such a pedigree warrants as within the realm of reason state convictions based on improperly obtained, *but incontestably reliable*, evidence. It requires little imagination to guess that Mr. Justice Frankfurter knows the dilemma which the great Mansfield described to David Garrick, "A judge on the bench is now and then in your whimsical situation between Tragedy and Comedy; inclination drawing one way and a long string of precedents the other."[73] That the Justice sometimes finds the clash between his heart's desire and the external standard other than whimsical there can be no doubt.[74] But that price must be paid if judicial review is to be a disciplined, objective instrument as little related as possible to the private policy preferences of those who for the moment sit upon the bench.

It is noteworthy that Mr. Justice Black did not dissent in *Wolf*. His deep libertarianism does not reveal itself in search and seizure cases.[75] Can it be that this unusual insensitivity springs from his experience as a congressional investigator; that here for once his idealism has yielded to mundane considerations? Perhaps he has come to believe that we may well improve a remedy that "punishes" the policeman by freeing the convict—that shields the guilty yet does nothing for the innocent whose privacy has been wrongfully invaded.

It is a striking fact that while President Roosevelt's "Court-packing plan" was widely opposed, few attempted to defend "the nine old men." They had misused judicial power to the detriment of democratic government. Mr. Justice Black apparently designed his "absolutes" to forestall repetition of the old abuse. But rules rigid enough to accomplish this would also, if followed, prevent the cure of what the Justice sees as present ills. Thus on occasion, as we have seen, he silently abandons his *Adamson* interpretation of the Fourteenth Amendment. Similarly, in the *Times-Mirror* case, without explanation, he gave up (temporarily) his view that corporations are not protected by the Fourteenth Amendment. After all, the "person" whose freedom to publish he there secured was a corporation. In the second "released-time" case he ran into another hitch.[76] Incorporation of the Bill of Rights into the Fourteenth Amendment is supposed to give the latter a "clearly defined" content.[77] Yet the only two judges—Black and Douglas—who nominally accept full incorporation could not agree with each other as to the legality of the *Zorach* released-time system. In fact they differ frequently as to the meaning of the Bill of Rights[78]—despite what they have called its "clearly marked boundaries."[79]

Plato's vexing problem—law versus discretion—is still with us. Repelled by the old "laissez-faire" abuse, Mr. Justice Black tries to purify and stabilize the law by clear, categoric rules. The purpose, plainly, is to minimize judicial discretion, provide a high degree of predictability as to the outcome of litigation, and leave basic policy changes to the democratic processes. But to curb judicial discretion is to curb its potential for good as well as for evil. Hence the wooden rules and their author's unwillingness to follow them. The Justice has not found a way to limit the discretion of other judges without limiting himself. Rejecting orthodox precepts and finding his own substitutes inadequate, he is left in difficult cases with little but *ad hoc* grounds for decision. In this impasse he is guided apparently by his own benevolent ideals—just as some of the "nine old men" were guided evidently by their more spartan principles.

Mr. Justice Frankfurter avoids this embarrassment. For him discretion is inevitable in constitutional decisions, because the basic law is necessarily imprecise. If uncertainty promotes anarchy, precision invites stagnation (or inconsistency). The Justice seeks an Aristotelian mean. He does not try to hide, or apologize for, the discretionary element in adjudication. Nor would he eliminate it with mechanistic rules. Rather, he would exercise it humbly—not in accordance with his own heart's desire, but by the guidance of an external standard. This takes several forms[80] but ultimately its essence is the reasonable man. Who is this creature? He is the same old pragmatic genius who made the common law one of the world's two great legal systems. He is simply a device whereby judges, when the law leaves room for doubt, seek out the common sense, the accepted values, the conscience of the community.

Mr. Justice Frankfurter presumably had more than the new Court in mind when he observed that

> The decisions in the cases that really give trouble rest on judgment, and judgment derives from the totality of a man's nature and experience. Such judgment will be exercised by two types of men, broadly speaking, but of course with varying emphasis—those who express their private views or revelations, deeming them, if not *vox dei,* at least *vox populi;* or those who feel strongly that they have no authority to promulgate law by their merely personal view and whose whole training and proved performance substantially insure that their conclusions reflect understanding of, and due regard for, law as the expression of the views and feelings that may fairly be deemed representative of the community as a continuing society.[81]

FREEDOM FROM RACIAL DISCRIMINATION

There is much to be learned on the nature of the judicial process from the Court's handling of racial discrimination. For years prior to the Civil War a southern aristocracy dominated the Democratic party—which in turn dominated the national government. Under those conditions the severe strictures of the *Dred Scott* decision[82] upon the Negroes' status is not surprising. Nor is the very different attitude of a later Court, most of whose members were appointed by President Lincoln and President Grant. Surely the idealism of the Emancipation Proclamation finds expression in *Strauder* v. *West Virginia* and *Ex parte Virginia.*[83] But idealistic revolutions have their Thermidors. The Separate-But-Equal decision of 1896 in *Plessy* v. *Ferguson*[84] doubtless reflected what C. V. Woodward has brilliantly described as "reunion and reaction."[85] After the war America's attention turned from slavery to industrial revolution and continental expansion. Just as the Court responded in the 1890's by surrendering to "laissez faire," it also responded with the *Plessy* retreat from its earlier, more idealistic, intimations. In the new setting old passions of war and reconstruction could only hinder the real business at hand: economic expansion. Here northern and southern Bourbons could agree. The Hayes-Tilden election crisis gave them an opportunity to unite and conquer—to call the tune of national policy. Despite the corruption of the Grant administration the southern upper crust abandoned Tilden and gave the Republicans another victory—in exchange for the promise of a share in the spoils. Conversely, when northern Republicanism had to choose between its Lincolnian ideal of human freedom and its Hamiltonian Whiggery, it chose the latter. It abandoned the Negro to save high tariffs, "hard" money, the national bank system, land grants, and other less reputable subsidies for business.

The Supreme Court does not follow election returns, but if it is to thrive, it must respect the social forces that determine election and other major political settlements. No court can long withstand the morals of its era! Thus after a customary judicial lag *Plessy*—like the *Income Tax, Knight,* and *Debs* decisions of the same vintage[86]—reflected the "bargain," the Great Compromise, of 1877. Northern business barons got control of the economy; southern whites got control of the Negro (and a few economic crumbs). The price of Reunion was legalized racialism and a heady measure of plutocracy.[87]

Separate-But-Equal, Substantive Due Process, and Dual Federalism (the legalisms of the Spirit of '77) permitted a comfortable few to play the economic game with loaded dice— until the New Deal revolution. Under the impact of the Great Depression and the rise of Hitler, America's attention returned from the values of the Gilded Age to fundamentals. "Laissez faire" was no longer an adequate sugarcoating for widespread poverty in a land of plenty. Nazi storm troops demonstrated the implications of racialism in terms that few were able to ignore. The free world revolted against the principle that a man may be harassed for his ancestry. As usual, the Supreme Court responded to the temper of the times. The economic crisis would not permit a gradual and dignified retreat from "laissez faire." That died ignominiously in the spring of 1937. A few months later the first great judicial blow fell upon racialism in the schools.[88] But here there was no pressing crisis, and perhaps the solution was not quite so obvious, or so widely acceptable. For whatever reason, the Court responded in the more decorous manner of the common law that gradually undermines before it destroys. First it insisted upon true (and rejected the traditional mock) equality.[89] Finally *Plessy* itself was abandoned—presumably on the ground that in the context of our time racial segregation and human freedom are incompatible.[90] There was no dissent, no separate opinion, no effort to evade the issue. Perhaps the best explanation is that no Justice was prepared to face history with the albatross of racialism upon him. If this guess is sound, the judges no doubt felt as they did because the momentum of public sentiment made them feel that way. The 1954 decisions then reflect the conscience of their day as surely as *Plessy* reflects the spirit of the 1890's. In each instance the ethos of the age, speaking through the Constitution, had its way with the Court. Thoreau explained this long ago: "It is always easy to infringe the law—but the Bedouins of the desert find it impossible to resist public opinion." Or in the words of Learned Hand:

> The law must have an authority supreme over the will of the individual, and such an authority can arise only from a background of social acquiescence, which gives it the voice of indefinitely greater numbers than those of its expositors. Thus, the law surpasses the deliverances of even the most exalted of its prophets; the momentum of its composite will alone makes it effective to coerce the individual and reconciles him to his subservience. The pious traditionalism of the law has its root in a sound conviction of this necessity; it must be content to lag behind the best inspiration of its time until it feels behind it the weight of such general acceptance as will give sanction to its pretension to unquestioned dictation.[91]

4 FEDERALISM: STATES' RIGHTS AND NATIONAL RIGHTS

There is nothing I more deprecate than the use of the Fourteenth Amendment beyond the absolute compulsion of its words to prevent the making of social experiments that an important part of the community desires, in the insulated chambers afforded by the several States, even though the experiments may seem futile or even noxious to me and those whose judgment I most respect.

OLIVER WENDELL HOLMES

I do not think the United States would come to an end if we lost our power to declare an Act of Congress void. I do think the Union would be imperiled if we could not make that declaration as to the laws of the several States. For one in my place sees how often a local policy prevails with those who are not trained to national views and how often action is taken that embodies what the Commerce Clause was meant to end.

OLIVER WENDELL HOLMES

*T*HE great problem of huge, continental nations is how to have unity without uniformity; how to avoid anarchy and yet retain sufficient local initiative to insure a rich and stimulating culture. Federalism seeks to solve this riddle by a constitutional divison of power between nation and states. But language has not been found, either here or abroad, to separate national and local authority by a line that will neither bend nor break. Conditions change, human foresight is limited, and men cannot agree. Thus all federal systems have built-in umpires—umpires whose job it is to settle, case by case, those inevitable conflicts which the basic law can deal with only in general, abstract terms. In the United States this burden has fallen largely upon the Supreme Court.

Having got rid of one central government in 1776, the thirteen states were reluctant to create another, yet they knew the advantages of a united front. Their first solution, then, under the Articles of Confederation was a league without central authority. State sovereignty carried the day and all but destroyed America. Local self-interest undermined the general welfare. Having learned the sad fate of a nation at the mercy of parochial interests, the Founding Fathers turned to central government. The essence of the Constitution is restraint upon the parts for the protection of the whole. This for some was, and is, a bitter pill. To assuage widespread apprehension, Madison argued in *The Federalist*, No. 46, that the new central government need not be feared: ". . . the first and most natural attachment of the people will be to the governments of their respective states." But with uncanny insight he added:

> If . . . the people should in future become more partial to the federal than to the State governments, the change can only result from such manifest and irresistible proofs of a better administration, as will overcome all their antecedent propensities. And in that case, the people ought not surely to be precluded from giving most of their confidence where they may discover it to be most due. . . .

The shift of popular confidence or partiality from state to nation, which the acute Madison anticipated, began with the Civil War and accelerated with the integrating effects of the industrial revolution. By the 1880's a sensitive foreign observer found that the

> political importance of the States is no longer what it was in the early days of the Republic. Although the States have grown enormously in wealth and population, they have declined relatively to the central government. The excellence of State laws and the merits of a State administration make less difference to the inhabitants than formerly, because the hand of the

National government is more frequently felt. The questions which the State deals with, largely as they influence the welfare of the citizen, do not touch his imagination like those which Congress handles, because the latter determine the relations of the republic to the rest of the world, and affect the area that lies between the two oceans. The State set out as an isolated and self-sufficing commonwealth. It is now merely a part of a far grander whole. . . .[1]

By 1948 another outsider spoke of the American state as "a province in which it is not difficult to distinguish what may perhaps be termed the vestigial remains of sovereign power."[2] Only yesterday Dennis Brogan, the latest British specialist in American affairs, noted the discrepancy between our professions and our practice. Judging by what we do, he said, and overlooking what we say, it is plain that Americans have less confidence in state than in national government. Why else do we turn so markedly from the one to the other when we want to get things done? After all, no one sits in Congress but representatives from the several states. Madison's "prophecy" has been fulfilled. Doubtless without meaning to do so, President Eisenhower's Commission on Intergovernmental Relations explained why this is so. To put it baldly, state government is inefficient and out-of-date. Still clinging verbally to cherished ideals of states' rights, we have learned from experience that the states have not been able to serve our modern needs. We have, in Madison's words, "become more partial to the federal than to the State governments . . . [a change which could] only result from . . . manifest and irresistible proofs of a better administration. . . ."

By its constant interference in the interest of "laissez faire," the old Court did much to undermine popular confidence in local authority. Of course it interfered with national government too, but (significantly) when the revolt came, it came at the national level. State government, for example, is still restrained by Substantive Due Process in the hands of *state courts*.[3] Another difficulty, as the Commission on Intergovernmental Affairs points out, is the outmoded—because inflexible—state constitutions. Finally, it has been observed:

> In state government are to be found in their most extreme and vicious forms all the worst evils of misrule in the country. Venality, open domination and manipulation by vested interests, unspeakable callousness in the care of the sick, aged and unfortunate, criminal negligence in law enforcement, crass deprivation of primary constitutional rights, obfuscation, obsolescence, obstructionism, incompetence, and even outright dictatorship are widespread characteristics.[4]

No doubt this is in part exaggeration, but few would deny its germ of truth.

In this setting the new Court has had to play its role as umpire between state and national authority. We have seen the views of Justices Black and Frankfurter on the scope of state power vis-à-vis trial procedure and freedom of expression and religion. Obviously, federalistic considerations were relevant—at least for Mr. Justice Frankfurter. He would leave the burden of local problems to the states, except in the extreme case where, in Holmes's words, rational and fair men "necessarily would admit that the [state measure] would infringe fundamental principles as they have been understood by the traditions of our people and our law." To paraphrase Mr. Justice Frankfurter in the *Uveges* and "flag salute" cases: at best, intervention by the Court in the governmental processes of the states is delicate business. It should be indulged in only when no reasonable doubt is left that the state has violated the Constitution. Intervention has all the disadvantages of outside interference. *It weakens local responsibility, which in the long run is the ultimate safeguard for freedom in local matters.*[5] Or, as Brandeis might have said, responsibility is the great developer of men—and states. In contrast, Mr. Justice Black finds in states' rights and local responsibility no, or little, weight vis-à-vis claims of civil liberty. In such cases, he insists, the Court has a special duty that is not discharged by finding state action within the realm of reason. Here the standard should be much higher; judicial tolerance the exception, not the rule. We turn now to more subtle problems in the relation of state and nation.

DIVERSITY JURISDICTION

Federal forms of government entail two distinct systems of legal rights: those created by the states and those created by the nation. Under a dual system of courts such as ours it would be logical to suppose that enforcement of state-created rights is a matter for state courts exclusively, while nationally created claims are reserved for federal tribunals. In fact there is overlap. Both national and state courts enforce both state and federal rights. Federal courts have jurisdiction of cases arising under national law. They also have jurisdiction of litigation arising exclusively under state law, provided certain selected classes of persons are involved.[6] Of the cases within the latter category, easily the most numerous are those which come into federal courts simply because the plaintiff is a citizen of one state and the defendant of another. This diversity of citizenship jurisdiction, as it is called, raises vexing problems in the division of authority between the two levels of government. For the

> stuff of diversity jurisdiction is state litigation. The availability of federal tribunals for controversies concerning matters which in themselves are outside federal power and exclusively within state authority, is the essence of a jurisdiction solely resting on the fact that a plaintiff and a defendant are citizens of different states. The power of Congress to confer such jurisdiction was based on the desire of the Framers to assure out-of-state litigants courts free from susceptibility to potential local bias.[7]

In such situations the federal courts sit, in effect, as special state courts where once we feared state tribunals might be biased against outsiders. From the beginning Congress has recognized the state capacity in which federal courts act in diversity cases. It has required them in such litigation to apply state "law." But long ago, in *Swift* v. *Tyson*,[8] the Supreme Court read this mandate to refer only to state legislative law.

Thus federal courts were free to ignore state common (i.e., decisional) law and to apply their own in diversity cases. The result was that, in the absence of state legislation, federal courts governed (i.e., formulated law) in matters which, by hypothesis, had been reserved to the states. Thus there arose within each state two separate common law legal systems with respect to purely local affairs. In many situations the law with respect to a given issue would vary, i.e., one's legal rights and duties varied, according to the court (state or federal) in which one's case arose. Shortly after the constitutional revolution of 1937, *Erie Rd. Co.* v. *Tompkins*[9] overruled the *Swift* decision. Federal court lawmaking for the states was held unconstitutional.

Under the new approach local affairs are to be governed by state law. But this is not quite as simple a matter as it may seem. Federal courts, of course, are entitled to follow their own procedures in enforcing state law. The difficulty is that the line between procedure and substance is not always clear. Or, to put it differently, procedure may affect substance. For example, legislation fixing the period within which law suits may be brought is generally considered a matter of procedure. Suppose, then, a person waits so long before bringing his case in a state court that it is outlawed by state law. Is he free to go into a federal court on "diversity" grounds and enjoy its longer period for bringing suits? This was the nub of *Guarantee Trust Co.* v. *York*.[10] In it, Mr. Justice Frankfurter laid out the Court's new approach, after *Erie* had demolished the rotten structure of *Swift* v. *Tyson*. Only Justices Rutledge and Murphy dissented. The new rule is simply that in diversity cases federal courts must follow *all state law*, whether procedural or substantive, which might affect the *outcome* of litigation. If under state law a party cannot win a case in a state court, he shall not win it in a federal court "a block away":

> *Erie R. Co.* v. *Tompkins* was not an endeavor to formulate scientific terminology [as to the distinction between procedure and substance]. It expressed a policy that touches vitally the proper distribution of judicial power between State and federal

courts. In essence, the intent of that decision was to insure that, in all cases where a federal court is exercising jurisdiction solely because of the diversity of citizenship of the parties, the outcome of the litigation in the federal court should be substantially the same, so far as legal rules determine the outcome of a litigation, as it would be if tried in a State court.

If state policy fixes the period within which local-law litigation may be brought, that policy prevails. One citizen shall not have advantage over another merely because his case happens to be triable in a federal court, while the other's is not. *Erie* and *York,* along with the destruction of Substantive Due Process, liberated the states from age-old shackles. Here is broad, "new" freedom—and responsibility—for local management of local affairs. This is a challenge to the states to wipe out the lethargy that has forced citizens to turn from them to Washington. Here is the opportunity to regain the respect that Madison warned the states would lose through inefficiency. Obviously the new states' rights is affirmative. It enables, and expects, the states to re-assume their proper role in American government. The old states' rights, it will be recalled, was essentially negative—a device for hamstringing national government.

For years, Mr. Justice Black and the Court accepted and applied the *York* principle without question. Then came the case of an injured workman, *Byrd* v. *Blue Ridge Rural Electric Cooperative.*[11] Byrd worked for a contractor who was building power lines for the co-op. Suffering an injury, he brought a common-law negligence action against the co-op in a federal court on diversity grounds. The common-law suit was permissible if Byrd was not a co-op employee within the meaning of the state workmen's compensation law. If he was such an "employee," his only recourse would be a workmen's compensation claim. The state law defined the employer-employee relationship rather broadly in an effort to give workers the benefit of any doubt as to compensation coverage. So, too, under state law, existence of the relationship for workmen's compensation purposes was a matter for decision by the trial judge, not by the jury. The Supreme Court, including Mr. Justice Black, refused to follow state law and ordered the employee relationship issue to be decided instead by jury:

> ... were "outcome" the only consideration a strong case might appear for saying that the federal court should follow the state practice.
>
> But there are affirmative countervailing considerations at work here. The federal system is an independent system for administering justice to litigants. . . . An essential characteristic of that system is the manner in which, in civil common-law actions, it distributes trial functions between judge and jury and, under the influence—if not the command—of the Seventh Amendment, assigns the decisions of disputed questions of fact to the jury. . . . Thus the inquiry here is whether the federal policy favoring jury decisions of disputed fact questions should yield to the state rule in the interest of furthering the objective that the litigation should not come out one way in the federal court and another way in the state court.
>
> We think that in the circumstances of this case the federal court should not follow the state rule.

What the crucial "circumstances" were is not explained. Presumably the reference is not to any special factual difficulty but to a "federal policy favoring jury decisions of disputed fact questions." But what fact issue was there? In the realm of fact Byrd was an employee of the contractor. This was undisputed. The issue was whether, for workmen's compensation purposes, he was a *statutory employee* of the co-op. In short, state law recognized this was a matter which could be resolved only by lawyer's learning, not by the kind of everyday factual experience within the competence of laymen on a jury. That is why under state law it was to be decided by a judge.

Since the Circuit Court of Appeals had found as a matter of state law that Byrd was a statutory employee of the co-op, his suit had been dismissed. Reversal by the Supreme Court gave him another go—another chance to get a much higher award from a jury than he could hope to get on a workmen's compensation claim. Shades of the FELA *certiorari* cases! Of course one's heart goes out to injured workmen. But the state in which this accident occurred had not been callous. It had abolished the old-fashioned, presumably unfair, negligence action and substituted modern workmen's compensation coverage for "employees." In the FELA *certiorari* cases Mr. Justice Black and others seem to use the well-known sympathies of the jury to evade the old law of negligence and achieve something like the assurance of workmen's compensation. Here they seem to use the same device to get around genuine workmen's compensation in favor of the potentially more remunerative negligence verdict. The common denominator apparently is a humane concern for the victims of industrial accidents. But the cost of *Byrd* is a step back towards *Swift* v. *Tyson* and the principle that each state shall have two different legal systems for purely local litigation. *Byrd*'s case is tried under one rule because by chance he and the defendant come from different states. Byrd's brother, suffering a like injury from the same accident, must have his case tried under a different rule—because perchance he and the defendant are citizens of the same state. Different rules invite different outcomes. State-made law will govern for one brother but not for the other in a situation that falls entirely outside the province of national affairs. Indeed, one brother will very likely win his case while the other loses.

Justices Frankfurter, Harlan, and Whittaker dissented (Burton, who had joined them in dissent in *Moore* v. *Terminal Rd. Ass'n. of St. Louis*,[12] was no longer on the bench). Mr. Justice Whittaker rested on the *Erie-York* rule. The others did not get that far. They saw no conflict of evidence for a jury to settle, even if state law was to be ignored in favor of a "federal policy."

Under the *York* "outcome" doctrine federal courts must follow, not make, state law. But what of a diversity suit as to which state law is obscure? In such a case involving Illinois alimony rules, Mr. Justice Frankfurter suggested a federal court ought to hold up decision for a reasonable time "while the plaintiff seeks with all deliberate speed a decision on the crucial question of the case in the Illinois courts."[13] His colleagues rejected the proposal out of hand, presumably because of the delays involved. This, the Justice pointed out, left formulation of *state* alimony law to a lower federal court, "which in the very nature of things can render only a tentative and indecisive judgment. Tentative and indecisive, because whatever view [the federal court] takes on this question may be authoritatively supplanted by the only court that can finally settle the issue, namely, the Supreme Court of Illinois."

Mr. Justice Black's solution is more direct. He would on occasion simply order the federal case dismissed. *Burford* v. *Sun Oil Company*[14] involved complex problems in oil and gas regulation under Texas law. Speaking for a bare majority, Mr. Justice Black in the exercise of what he called "equitable discretion" told the lower federal courts to dismiss the suit. Four judges speaking through Mr. Justice Frankfurter bitterly dissented:

> It is the essence of diversity jurisdiction that federal judges and juries pass on asserted claims because the result might be different if they were decided by a state court. [This was before the *York* decision.] There may be excellent reasons why Congress should abolish diversity jurisdiction. But, with all deference, it is not a defensible ground for having this Court by indirection abrogate diversity jurisdiction when, as a matter of fact, Congress has persistently refused to restrict such jurisdiction except in the limited area occupied by the Johnson Act. The Congressional premise of diversity jurisdiction is that the unfairness against outside litigants is to be avoided by providing the neutral forum of a federal court. The Court today is in effect withdrawing this grant of jurisdiction in order to avoid possible unfairness against state interests in the federal courts.

A few months later Mr. Justice Frankfurter's view prevailed. *Burford* was narrowly confined, if not abandoned: "Congress having adopted the policy of opening the federal courts to suitors in . . . diversity cases . . . , we can discern in its action no recognition of a policy which would exclude cases from the jurisdiction merely because they involve state law or because the law is uncertain or difficult to determine."[15] Justices Black and Jackson dissented.

There are other dilemmas in diversity jurisdiction. In a concurring opinion in *Lumbermen's Mutual Casualty Co.* v. *Elbert*,[16] Mr. Justice Frankfurter observed:

> ... our holding results in such a glaring perversion of the purpose to which the original grant of diversity jurisdiction was directed that it ought not to go without comment, as further proof of the mounting mischief inflicted on the federal judicial system by the unjustifiable continuance of diversity jurisdiction.

The case arose in Louisiana, where state appellate courts (due to the influence of the old French civil law) have much broader power to review jury verdicts than do federal appellate courts. Thus, notwithstanding the heroic effort in *York,* differences in "outcome" in state and federal courts on the same issue are still possible. As Mr. Justice Frankfurter pointed out:

> [Louisiana] plaintiffs in negligence suits have suddenly found the federal courts their protectors and insurance companies have discovered the virtues of the state courts. In New York, insurance companies run to cover in the federal courts and plaintiffs feel outraged by the process of attrition in enforcing their claims, due to a delay of from three to four years before a case can come to trial. As to both situations, the vice is the availability of diversity jurisdiction. What is true of New York is true, in varying degrees, of every big center.

More is involved, however, than the selfishness of litigants in exploiting the law's weaknesses, and more than states' rights. Mr. Justice Frankfurter said:

> My concern is with the bearing of diversity jurisdiction on the effective functioning of the federal judiciary. [In dissent below, Judge Rives] stated with impressive bluntness the effect on the work of the federal and state courts in allowing diversity jurisdiction to be put to such purposes: ... "Continued consideration ... has convinced me that there is something fundamentally wrong with our legal theories when they permit the great bulk of the casualty damage suit litigation in Louisiana to clog

the dockets of the federal court, while, I understand, some of the state judges actually do not have enough litigation to keep them busy."

We have seen that however distasteful Mr. Justice Frankfurter finds diversity jurisdiction, he cannot bring himself to evade.it. Shunning his colleague's do-it-yourself technique in *Burford,* his remarks in the *Lumbermen's* case are plainly addressed to Congress. The shafts struck home. Quoting him, a congressional committee in 1958 recommended, and Congress passed, a measure drastically reducing diversity jurisdiction.[17] Instead of undertaking a bit of wholesale judicial legislation, Mr. Justice Frankfurter (among others) year after year urged Congress to do the job. The contrasting methods of the two Justices could hardly be more starkly revealed.

A few years before these events, Congress had expanded diversity jurisdiction by providing, in effect, that the District of Columbia should be considered a "state" for diversity purposes. In the realm of laymen's affairs this was not unreasonable. It gave to citizens of the District of Columbia a status that other citizens have long enjoyed. But the effect was to broaden further the authority of federal courts in purely local affairs. *National Mutual Ins. Co.* v. *Tidewater Transfer Company*[18] raised the question of whether Congress had constitutional power to extend diversity jurisdiction in controversies between a citizen of the District and a state citizen. The constitutional language in Article III which authorizes diversity jurisdiction refers to controversies "between citizens of different states." It had been settled since Chief Justice Marshall's day that the District of Columbia is not a state for diversity purposes. The *Tidewater* case is particularly interesting because it demonstrates that Mr. Justice Frankfurter does not find all parts of the Constitution equally flexible:

> The precision which characterizes these portions of Article III is in striking contrast to the imprecision of so many other provisions of the Constitution dealing with other very vital aspects of government. This was not due to chance or ineptitude on

the part of the Framers. The differences in subject matter account for the drastic differences in treatment. Great concepts like "Commerce . . . among the several states," "due process of law," "liberty," "property," were purposely left to gather meaning from experience. For they relate to the whole domain of social and economic fact, and the statesmen who founded this Nation knew too well that only a stagnant society remains unchanged. But when the Constitution in turn gives strict definition of power or specific limitations upon it we cannot extend the definition or remove the translation. . . .

There was deep distrust of a federal judicial system, as against the State judiciaries, in the Constitutional Convention. This distrust was reflected in the evolution of Article III. Moreover, when they dealt with the distribution of judicial power as between the courts of the States and the courts of the United States, the Framers were dealing with a technical subject in a professional way. . . . The Framers guarded against the self-will of the courts as well as against the will of Congress by marking with exactitude the outer limits of federal judicial power. . . .

If there is one subject as to which this Court ought not to feel inhibited in passing on the validity of legislation by doubts of its own competence to judge what Congress has done, it is legislation affecting the jurisdiction of federal courts. When Congress on a rare occasion through inadvertence or generosity exceeds those limitations, this Court should not good-naturedly ignore such a transgression. . . .

Here is one of the very rare occasions on which Mr. Justice Frankfurter has voted to strike down an act of Congress. A majority of the Court agreed that Article III outlawed what Congress had done. A different majority also agreed with the Justice that the measure was not authorized by anything in Article I which gives Congress power to govern the District of Columbia. Yet the differing minorities on these two questions constituted a third majority which upheld the challenged act of Congress. As Mr. Justice Frankfurter put it:[19]

A substantial majority of the Court agrees that each of the two grounds urged in support of the attempt by Congress to extend diversity jurisdiction to cases involving citizens of the

District of Columbia must be rejected—but not the same majority. And so, conflicting minorities in combination bring to pass a result—paradoxical as it may appear—which differing majorities of the Court find insupportable.

Mr. Justice Black was one of the minority that rested on the Article I power. In this view, supported by only three members of the Court, a power denied by the specific provisions of Article III was granted by the generality of Article I. If this seems arbitrary, its effect was to treat citizens of the District of Columbia equally with citizens of the states—at the expense of expanding a troublesome jurisdiction.

FEDERAL QUESTION JURISDICTION

For almost a hundred years we relied upon state courts (subject to review by the Supreme Court) for the protection of most rights arising under national law. Then in 1875, apparently in response to the nationalizing influence of the Civil War, Congress first gave the lower federal courts general authority—concurrently with state tribunals—to decide cases involving federal-right questions. One purpose of the change was to attain sympathetic enforcement of rights insured by the Civil War amendments against state interference. Serious difficulty arose with the advent of Substantive Due Process. An amendment, presumably designed to deal with the problems of newly freed slaves, became a "laissez-faire" limitation upon state economic policy. A flood of federal lower court injunctions seriously impeded the processes of local government. Congress reacted with a series of measures modifying in various ways what it had granted in 1875. In 1910 it required the convening of a special three-judge court for the issuance of certain injunctions and allowed direct appeals to the Supreme Court. Such legislation was clarified and extended from time to time thereafter. In 1913 an abortive provision was made for the stay of federal injunction proceedings upon institution of state court test cases. The essential ineffectiveness of these measures resulted in 1934 in substantial elimination of federal jurisdiction to enjoin state public utility rate orders. Three years later similar restraints were imposed upon injunctions against collection of state taxes. This saved for state adjudication, in the first instance, the two major areas where federal injunctions had been most obnoxious, but other areas remained vulnerable.

Meanwhile, the Supreme Court, like Congress, showed misgivings concerning this aspect of government by injunction. Drawing upon the traditional discretion of the chancellor, Mr. Justice Holmes introduced a series of self-imposed judicial restraints that culminated in Mr. Justice Frankfurter's famous doctrine of abstention. Whereas the earlier cases turned rather narrowly upon the availability of adequate state remedies, the new emphasis is upon the nature of the state policy at issue. The classic case is *Railroad Commission* v. *Pullman*.[20] The commission had issued an administrative order which was challenged as discriminatory against Negroes. Its enforcement was enjoined by a federal trial court. On review the Supreme Court, via Mr. Justice Frankfurter, found southern racial problems "a sensitive area of social policy on which the federal courts ought not to enter unless no alternative to . . . adjudication is open." An alternative was found in the vagueness of state law as to whether the offending order had in fact been authorized. Reluctant, as usual, to interpret state legislation—such interpretation can only be a "forecast rather than a determination"—Mr. Justice Frankfurter led a unanimous Court to vacate the injunction. But it is crucial that here, unlike *Burford*, the trial court was ordered to retain the case until the state courts had had a reasonable opportunity to settle the state-law question. "The resources of equity are equal to an adjustment that will avoid the waste of a tentative decision as well as the friction of a premature constitutional adjudication."

Temporary abstention, i.e., postponement, is one thing; refusal to adjudicate is another. To the extent that the jurisdictional principle of 1875 stands unmodified by subsequent legislation, federal equitable relief against state action must be available—or so it seems to Mr. Justice Frankfurter. In *Ala-*

bama Public Service Commission v. *Southern Ry. Co.,*[21] the commission had refused to permit abandonment of certain "uneconomic" train facilities. The railroad, claiming deprivation of property without due process of law, sought injunctive relief. The Court held that federal jurisdiction should not be exercised lest the domestic policy of the state be obstructed; this in the name of equitable discretion.

Justices Frankfurter and Jackson concurred in the Court's result, for they found no merit in the railroad's claim. But they objected vigorously to the proposition that federal courts may refuse to exercise jurisdiction conferred in a valid act of Congress:

> By one fell swoop the Court now finds that Congress indulged in needless legislation in the acts of 1910, 1913, 1925, 1934 and 1937. By these measures, Congress, so the Court [in effect] now decides, gave not only needless but inadequate relief, since it now appears that the federal courts have inherent power to sterilize the Act of 1875 against all proceedings challenging local regulation.

A most revealing recent case is *Textile Workers Union* v. *Lincoln Mills.*[22] The Taft-Hartley Act gave the federal courts jurisdiction over "suits for violation of contracts between an employer and a labor organization representing employees in an industry affecting commerce." On its face this merely provides a federal forum; it does not establish any law (rights) for the federal judges to enforce. How can judges exercise jurisdiction to enforce national rights when Congress has created none? The Court held that Congress had intended the federal judiciary to "fashion" an appropriate law of labor-management contracts.[23] In short, congressional power to grant federal-question authority to federal courts is now apparently so broad that Congress need not create, or specify, the right to be enforced.

The *Lincoln Mills* decision authorizes a whole new body of federal "common law" which, as Mr. Justice Frankfurter pointed out in dissent, leads to one of the following "incongruities":

> (1) conflict in federal and state court interpretations of collective bargaining agreements; (2) displacement of state law by federal law in state courts . . . in all actions regarding collective bargaining agreements; or (3) exclusion of state court jurisdiction over these matters.[24]

The Justice's elaborate examination of the legislative history of the provision in question suggests that Congress' purpose was merely to make unions *suable*.[25] With a few exceptions, the lawmakers seemed unaware of the technical problems of federal jurisdiction involved—to say nothing of the delegation of lawmaking power to judges. To avoid these constitutional difficulties, Mr. Justice Frankfurter was prepared to read the Taft-Hartley provision as concerned with diversity, rather than federal question, jurisdiction. This would satisfy what presumably was Congress' major purpose—the suability of unions. It would also leave intact the states' traditional authority in the realm of contract law. (As we have seen, the *Erie* and *York* decisions require federal courts in diversity cases to follow state decisional rules.) Here again Mr. Justice Frankfurter could not lightly accept the principle of wholesale judicial legislation. If Congress wants to displace the states from areas which they have customarily occupied, let it do so knowingly and explicitly. And let it do its own lawmaking and not leave that to federal judges. Does *Lincoln Mills* suggest that if Congress granted jurisdiction over interstate divorce cases, the federal courts would be authorized to fashion a national law for the dissolution of marriages?

There is a common problem behind most of these federal question and diversity cases. Congress has not clearly defined the bounds between state and federal court competence. It has the power to do so but for the most part has left the matter for solution by judges on a case-by-case basis. A careful student has suggested that "In any new revision [of the Judicial Code] the legislators would do well to remember that the allocation of power to the federal courts should be limited to those matters in which their expertise in federal law might be used, leaving to the state judiciaries the primary obligation of pronouncing state law."²⁶ Obviously, the goal here proposed is the guiding principle in Mr. Justice Frankfurter's opinions—to the extent that Congress leaves the problem to judicial discretion. The same rule of specialization and division of labor guides him in the FELA *certiorari* cases, in the administrative law area, and indeed in the whole realm of judicial review. Mr. Justice Black no doubt concurs in principle but is more apt to make exceptions to achieve a generous and "just" result. He will not be "fooled by technicalities."

FEDERAL REVIEW OF STATE DECISIONS

With few exceptions, Congress has not given federal courts *exclusive* authority to enforce rights arising under federal law. To put it differently, state and federal courts have concurrent jurisdiction with respect to most claims of federal right. To insure uniformity in the meaning of national law, however, state interpretations are subject to Supreme Court review. It may be noted, parenthetically, that to evade "desegregation" an ex-Justice and former southern governor has urged Congress to abolish this reviewing authority.²⁷ The result, of course, would be that federal law inevitably would mean different things in different states. It would also probably mean different things within the same state—depending upon what court (state or federal) rendered decision.

We consider here only a few of many problems involved in this crucial federal-state relationship. The first is that enforcement of national law in state litigation raises in reverse the old diversity puzzle of the relation of procedure to substance. Subject to certain constitutional restraints in favor of fair trials, each level of government is free to devise its own judicial procedures. Litigants who choose to assert federal claims in a state court go into that court subject to its rules of procedure. A similar canon applies to those who press state claims in federal tribunals, e.g., in diversity cases. In an FELA controversy the state court followed established state procedure by construing a vague complaint "most strongly against" the complainant.[28] In other words the burden of pleading clearly rested upon the pleader by state law. The result was that the plaintiff's case was dismissed. Mr. Justice Black led a reversing majority: "Strict local rules of pleading cannot be used to impose unnecessary burdens upon rights of recovery authorized by federal law." Here, as in the *Byrd* case,[29] another element of state procedure was subsumed to federal judge-made law. Justices Frankfurter and Jackson dissented:

> One State may cherish formalities more than another, one State may be more responsive than another to procedural reforms. If a litigant chooses to enforce a Federal right in a State court, he cannot be heard to object if he is treated exactly as are plaintiffs who press like claims arising under State law with regard to the form in which the claim must be stated—the particularity, for instance, with which a cause of action must be described. Federal law, though invoked in a State court, delimits the Federal claim—defines what gives a right to recovery and what goes to prove it. But the form in which the claim must be stated need not be different from what the State exacts in the enforcement of like obligations created by it, so long as a requirement does not add to, or diminish, the right as defined by Federal law, nor burden the realization of this right in the actualities of litigation.

Another problem in the area of federal-state relationships is this: what constitutes reversible error in a state decision? *Terminiello* v. *Chicago*[30] involved a conviction for disorderly conduct under a local ordinance. The conduct in question was a speech. The accused did not object to the trial court's charge to the jury that discourse "may constitute a breach of the peace if it stirs the public to anger, invites dispute, brings about a condition of unrest. . . ." For present purposes it may be assumed that this charge so narrowly limited speech as to violate the federal Constitution. Though the accused raised many other objections, he did not object on this crucial point at any stage of the proceedings. That is, he did not claim in any of the four courts through which his case progressed that the jury charge had denied him any federal right. Indeed, he explicitly disclaimed any such objection in argument before the Supreme Court. His whole position in all four hearings focused on the nature and circumstances of the talk. Our adversary trial system rests on the premise that litigants *present* issues for adjudication. The whole purpose of pleading is to weed out those matters on which the parties agree, and to frame sharply the issues for decision.

The Supreme Court's function in the *Terminiello* case was to review the decision of Illinois' highest court. Had the latter erred? Recall that no claim of federal right on the crucial point had been presented to it—and none had been adjudged. Thus its decision was free of reversible error in the traditional sense. Terminiello's lawyers, however, had been at "fault" (as a matter of hindsight) in not raising what turned out to be the decisive issue. If the Supreme Court's function were not merely to correct challenged mistakes in judgments under review but also to correct the "errors" of litigants, the burden would be unbearable. If counsels' lapses are to be corrected in some cases (only a $100.00 fine was involved in *Terminiello*) and not in others, the result could hardly be called fair to all concerned. It has been observed that "We cannot have equal justice under law, except we have some law." On the other hand, must a litigant suffer because he failed to anticipate a vital issue? Here, perhaps, is the classic clash of individual interest and general principle; the hard case that invites bad law. The Court, obviously out of respect for free speech, held for the accused.

Mr. Justice Frankfurter, along with Chief Justice Vinson and Justices Jackson and Burton, could not agree that Terminiello should have special consideration:

> For the first time in the course of the 130 years in which state prosecutions have come here for review, this Court is today reversing a sentence imposed by a State court on a ground that

was urged neither here nor below and that was explicitly disclaimed on behalf of the petitioner at the bar of this Court. . . .

We have no authority to meddle with such a judgment unless some claim under the Constitution or the laws of the United
States have been made before the State court whose judgment
we are reviewing and unless the claim has been denied by that
court. How could there be a denial of a federal claim by the
Illinois courts . . . [if] no such claim was made? The relation of
the United States [and its courts] to the States [and their
courts] is a very delicate matter. It is too delicate to permit
silence when a judgment of a State court is reversed in disregard of the duty of this Court to leave untouched an adjudication of a State unless that adjudication is based upon a claim
of federal right which the State has had an opportunity to
meet and to recognize. . . . This is a court of review. . . . We do
not sit like a kadi under a tree dispensing justice according to
considerations of individual expediency.

A related issue arose in *Adler* v. *Board of Education of New
York*[31] concerning a schoolteacher loyalty law. Six members of
the Court found the measure valid. Justices Black and Douglas
thought it unconstitutional:

> The present law proceeds on a principle repugnant to our
> society—guilt by association. A teacher is disqualified because
> of her membership in an organization found to be "sub-
> versive." The finding as to the subversive character of the
> organization is made in a proceeding to which the teacher is
> not a party and in which it is not clear that she may even be
> heard. To be sure she may have a hearing when charges of
> disloyalty are leveled against her. But in that hearing the find-
> ing as to the "subversive" character of the organization ap-
> parently may not be reopened in order to allow her to show
> the truth of the matter. . . . She may, it is said, show her inno-
> cence. But innocence in this case turns on knowledge; and
> when the witch-hunt is on, one who must rely on ignorance
> leans on a feeble reed.
>
> The very threat of such a procedure is certain to raise havoc
> with academic freedom.

It will be noted that the dissenters find invalidity in things that
may or may not happen and in others which are asserted as

"certain" to happen. None of the evils feared had transpired; the state had not yet attempted to enforce the law.

Accordingly, Mr. Justice Frankfurter thought the case should be dismissed as premature. The loyalty program was still in the blueprint stage. Its machinery had not been set in motion:

> We are asked to adjudicate claims against its constitutionality before the scheme has been put into operation, before the limits that it imposes upon free inquiry and association, the scope of scrutiny that it sanctions, and the procedural safeguards that will be found to be implied for its enforcement have been authoritatively defined. I think we should adhere to the teaching of this Court's history to avoid constitutional adjudications on merely abstract or speculative issues and to base them on the concreteness afforded by an actual, present, defined controversy, appropriate for judicial judgment, between adversaries immediately affected by it.

Could the difference between judicial pragmatism and idealism be more sharply focused than in this case? Mr. Justice Black was prepared to strike down a state law before anyone had been hurt, before anyone had an opportunity to see how, in fact, it would be administered. He would destroy what seemed to him an evil thing before it had a chance to spread its venom. Mr. Justice Frankfurter thought that since no one had been injured, state administrative and judicial agencies should have an opportunity to devise appropriate procedures, and correct faults (if any existed) before the federal courts intruded upon local policy. For him states' rights entails states' responsibilities.

NATIONAL AND STATE POWER WITH RESPECT TO INTERSTATE COMMERCE

The Constitution authorizes Congress to "regulate commerce among the several states."[32] This, Chief Justice Marshall held, was the power to "govern" not merely transportation of merchandise across state lines but any "intercourse" which "concerns more states than one."³³ The thought surely was that what affects only one state is that state's business. But, however local the *cause*, what *affects* more than a single state becomes national business. "If it is interstate commerce which feels the pinch, it does not matter how local the operation which applies the squeeze." This reflects experience under the Articles of Confederation which failed, among other reasons, because it provided no central authority to deal with domestic problems of general, or multistate, significance. Marshall's view has prevailed throughout our history—except between 1895 and 1937, as we have seen, with respect to "reputable" business interests. The New Deal judicial "revolution" simply wiped out that exception. It restored the national commerce power to pre-1895 status, a status which has *always* been recognized in cases not controlled by "laissez-faire" principles.³⁴ Since 1936 the Court has struck down no act of Congress on Commerce Clause grounds. Mr. Justice Frankfurter, however, has warned that

> The interpenetrations of modern society have not wiped out state lines. It is not for us to make inroads upon our federal system either by indifference to its maintenance or excessive regard for the unifying forces of modern technology. Scholastic reasoning may prove that no activity is isolated within the boundaries of a single state, but that cannot justify absorption of legislative power by the United States over every activity.³⁵

Such precautionary language, rare indeed in the past two decades, is simply another segment of a common thread in the Justice's opinions: within their insulated chambers the states are still responsible agencies in the pattern of American government. Justices Black, Douglas, and Murphy, though concurring in the result, seemed at pains to disassociate themselves from their colleague's language.

There is only one case since 1936 in which a Commerce Clause regulation has been seriously questioned within the Court. An act of Congress prohibits interstate shipment of gambling devices and requires dealers in such goods to report all sales and deliveries. In the absence of any forbidden inter-state shipment, the government charged certain dealers with failure to report. Justices Frankfurter, Jackson, and Minton, in *United States* v. *Five Gambling Devices*,[36] questioned "the power of Congress to enact legislation penalizing failure to report information concerning acts not shown to be in, or mingled with, or found to affect [interstate] commerce." To avoid this constitutional question they gave Congress the bene-fit of doubt by assuming the act was not intended to apply in such questionable circumstances. Justices Black and Douglas disassociated themselves from this reasoning but joined in the result on "self-incrimination" grounds. Chief Justice Warren and Justices Reed, Burton, and Clark dissented. In their view the act was valid even when applied in the circumstances of this case.

Apart from the qualms of Justices Frankfurter, Jackson, and Minton, the main problem since 1936 has been not the scope of the national commerce power but the effect of congressional legislation upon the states. The Constitution makes national law supreme.[37] This means that when a congressional and a state measure clash the former prevails, i.e., to the extent of the conflict the latter is wiped out. So much is elementary. Dis-agreement comes on whether a particular local measure in fact collides with a particular national measure. Of course each case presents its own peculiar circumstances. What is found in one is generally of little value in deciding another. Still the tilt of a judge's mind, or attitude, makes a difference. "In law too the emphasis makes the song." Thus in cases where a divided Court finds incompatibility, Mr. Justice Black generally votes against the state. He believes in states' rights—but not when civil liberty or national regulations are involved.

When there is room for doubt, Mr. Justice Frankfurter, on the other hand, will generally be found on the side upholding local government. This, of course, is mainly a matter of inter-preting the meaning of Congress:

To construe federal legislation so as not needlessly to forbid pre-existing state authority is to respect our federal system. Any indulgence in construction should be in favor of the states, because Congress can speak with drastic clarity whenever it chooses to assure full federal authority, completely displacing the states. [Moreover since] Congress can, if it chooses, entirely displace the states to the full extent of the far-reaching Commerce Clause, Congress needs no help from generous judicial implications to achieve supersession of State authority.[38]

To require the various agencies of the government who are the effective authors of legislation like that now before us to express clearly and explicitly their purpose in dislodging constitutional powers of states—if such is their purpose—makes for care in draftsmanship and for responsibility in legislation. To hold, as do the majority, that paralysis of state power is somehow to be found in the vague implications . . . [of federal enactments] is to encourage slipshodness in draftsmanship and irresponsibility in legislation.[39]

Hill v. *Florida*[40] illustrates the problem. State law required a $1.00 license for each labor-union business agent. A license could be issued only to a person of good moral character, who had not been convicted of felony, and who had been a citizen for more than ten years. The question was: did this provision conflict with the National Labor Relations Act? Mr. Justice Black for the Court found conflict: the purpose of the national act was to protect the "full freedom" of workers in the selection of bargaining agents. As Justices Frankfurter and Roberts saw it in dissent,

. . . Congress by protecting employees in their right to choose representatives for collective bargaining free from the coercion or influence of employers did not [expressly or] impliedly wipe out the right of States under their police power to require qualifications appropriate for union officials having fiduciary duties.

Congress had not explicitly provided either way. Most likely it had not even seen the problem. Thus neither "interpretation" was clearly right or wrong. Yet such cases demand decision.

Doubtless a judge's outcome depends upon his premise as to the relative roles of courts and legislatures in American government.

When a case of this kind involves not interstate commerce but Communist subversion, it is bound to reach the headlines. In *Pennsylvania* v. *Nelson*[41] a state trial court had found the accused guilty, *under state law*, of subversion *against the United States*. On review both Justices Black and Frankfurter shared the Supreme Court's view that federal law had taken over the field of subversion against the United States. It followed that state competence in this area had been displaced in favor of national policy. Some headlines complained that not only had the Supreme Court intruded upon states' rights, it had also freed a Communist convict. What the Court's attackers seldom bothered to explain was that the highest court of Pennsylvania had already struck down the state conviction. The federal Court merely affirmed that judgment. Here is what the *state* court said: "Sedition against the United States is not a local offense. It is a crime against the *Nation*. . . . It is not only important but vital that such prosecutions should be exclusively within the control of the Federal Government. . . ." Chief Justice Warren's opinion for the Supreme Court rests on several grounds. One of them, ignored by critics, was a statement by J. Edgar Hoover disclosing an attitude which may not unreasonably be attributed to Congress whose laws, after all, are supreme:

> The fact must not be overlooked that meeting the spy, the saboteur and the subverter is a problem that must be handled on a nation-wide basis. An isolated incident in the middlewest may be of little significance, but when fitted into a national pattern of similar incidents, it may lead to an important revelation of subversive activity. It is for this reason that the President requested all of our citizens and law enforcing agencies to report directly to the Federal Bureau of Investigation. . . .

Pennsylvania v. *Nelson* is important because it illustrates how easily critics may distort the significance of Court de-

cisions for partisan purposes. There can be no doubt that a
major part of the uproar that grew out of the *Nelson* case was
inspired by those who sought "revenge" for the desegregation
decisions by suggesting that the Court was communistic. The
Justices do not hold press conferences; they have no way to
set the record straight, to explain, or to argue their views in
the headlines. The *Nelson* decision could hardly be called an
intrusion upon states' rights: it *upheld* the decision of the
Pennsylvania Supreme Court. It did not set a Communist free;
it left him where he was—in a federal penitentiary.[42] It did
not involve interpretation of the Constitution but merely of an
act of Congress. Thus, whenever Congress chooses, it can open
to the states the power to outlaw and prosecute subversion
against the national government. Though the world had notice
of the problem some seven years ago when the Pennsylvania
Supreme Court published its decision, Congress has not seen
fit to change the law—if it does not, in fact, agree with J.
Edgar Hoover, the highest court of Pennsylvania, and the
Supreme Court of the United States. Indeed, it has been vigorously urged to make the change and has refused to do so.

The cases just considered involve the scope of state power
in the face of congressional legislation. Suppose Congress has
not acted. Shall the states then be free, for example, to regulate
and tax interstate commerce? The Constitution simply does
not say. Here is a fertile source of litigation. Our economy is
not divided into fifty neat and separate local packages, plus
one national package. Interstate commerce is merely a series
of local incidents—some of which inevitably pinch local affairs.
On the other hand, state taxation and regulation may be used
to give local interests an advantage over outside claims. Moreover, interstate business is a rich base for state taxation. It also
has special political charm: local taxes levied on it fall in large
measure on people in other states. This is a legislator's dream
—a rich source of tax revenue, the burden of which largely hits
those who cannot vote him out of office. Here, in short, is the
old problem of taxation without representation—the very

thing that destroyed the Articles of Confederation. To avoid a repetition of this experience was a major purpose of the Constitution.

The effort of the Founders has not been without success. Indeed one school of economic thought finds the genius of American industry not in Big Technology but in the Big Free Market. In this view the former arose and thrives mainly because of the latter. As Mr. Justice Jackson has it:

> Our system, fostered by the Commerce Clause, is that every farmer and every craftsman shall be encouraged to produce by the certainty that he will have free access to every market in the Nation, that no home embargoes will withhold his exports, and no . . . state will by customs, duties or regulations exclude them. Likewise, every consumer may look to the free competition from every producing area in the Nation to protect him from exploitation by any. Such was the vision of the Founders.[43]

And such, indeed, is the vision towards which, after centuries, Europe still struggles. What market freedom we have comes to us largely through the efforts of the Supreme Court.

> It is easy to mock or minimize the significance of "free trade among the states" . . . which is the significance given by a century and a half of adjudication in this Court. With all doubts as to what lessons history teaches, few seem clearer than the beneficial consequences which have flowed from this conception of the Commerce Clause [as a negative upon the states].[44]

Just as the Court has found in the Fourteenth Amendment and the Bill of Rights a base for balancing the claims of the individual as against those of government, so it has found in the Commerce Clause[45] a basic authority for mediating between state and nation. As we have seen, Mr. Justice Black would leave the problem to Congress, except in the case of outright discrimination against national intercourse. This would put the inertia of the national legislature—the difficulty of moving it to action—on the side of local freedom to regulate and tax. Here is the greatest, perhaps the only significant, respect that the Justice demonstrates for states' rights. But here, too, he wavers, at least when a state attempts to segregate citizens on racial grounds.[46] Indeed, he seems finally to have abandoned his "leave-it-to-Congress" gambit.[47]

Mr. Justice Jackson, at the opposite extreme, would put the inertia of Congress on the side of freedom for the national market. Any state measure in the interstate commercial area would be suspect, if not presumptively invalid. For usually state encroachments on interstate affairs "are individually too petty, too diversified, and too local to get the attention of a Congress hard pressed with more urgent matters. The practical result is that in default of action by us they will go on suffocating and retarding and Balkanizing American commerce, trade and industry."[48]

Between these extremes Mr. Justice Frankfurter (and perhaps most of his colleagues) finds "the basic function of this Court as the mediator of powers within the federal system."[49] In litigation involving impositions upon interstate commerce, the Justice follows the same balancing-of-interests technique that he uses in other cases. The claims of a national market must be weighed against those of local self-government. On the one side is the danger of Balkanization; on the other the scourge of outside interference with local affairs. In a case in which Mr. Justice Jackson wrote for the Court, his colleague Frankfurter felt "constrained to dissent because [he could not] agree in treating what is essentially a problem of striking a balance between competing interests as an exercise in absolutes. Nor does it seem . . . that such a problem should be disposed of on a record from which we cannot tell what weights to put in which side of the scales."[50]

In fact, the views of Justices Black and Jackson have failed to secure majority backing. But for a brief period Mr. Justice Rutledge seemed to have Court support for his multiple-burden rule in state tax cases. Eschewing both extremes, as did Mr. Justice Frankfurter, Rutledge wanted a "precise" guide between them. He found it in a *mechanistic* rule that, discrimination aside, any state tax on interstate trade must be upheld unless it is such that another state could repeat it.[51] In a word, just as states may tax the incidents of local business, so may they tax the corresponding, local incidents of national business. Only multistate incidents would be protected directly by the Commerce Clause, and only to the extent that taxes thereon would have to be apportioned among the states in which the multistate taxable event occurs. The multiple-burden rule has great appeal for those who like apparent precision, but it weights the scales rather heavily in favor of local affairs. The several states in which an interstate business operates are apt to put more localized burdens upon it than would be imposed upon a competing local business by the one state in which it functions. To protect each individual incident of interstate trade from multiple taxation does not necessarily result in the protection of interstate trade itself from cumulative burdens. Moreover, the "immunities implicit in the Commerce Clause and the potential taxing power of a State can hardly be made to depend, in the world of practical affairs, on the shifting incidence of the varying tax laws of the various States at a particular moment."[52] Accordingly, for all its vaunted realism, the Rutledge rule dealt, for the most part, only with hypothetically possible, not actual, multiple burdens. It treated all taxes as fungible, ignoring the fact that two or more cumulative interstate taxes may indeed be less burdensome than a single localized tax. It appears to have meant that, absent obvious discrimination in favor of local trade, any state could tax any aspect of interstate commerce, provided it pick an incident occurring exclusively within its own boundaries. This is a bit like trying to save a forest by partially protecting only those trees which straddle state lines—all others being left to the proven appetites of the residents of the respective states in which they grow.

The short of it is that, as the history of all the great English-speaking federal systems demonstrates, the interrelations between national and local levels of government raise questions that cannot be settled by thumb-rules:

We have considered literally scores of cases [involving state burdens on interstate commerce]. Whatever may be the generalities to which these cases gave utterance and about which there has been, on the whole, relatively little disagreement, the fate of state legislation in these cases has not been determined by these generalities but by the weight of the circumstances and the practical and experienced judgment in applying these generalities to the particular instances.[53]

Of course, the fact, or possibility, of multiple burdens must be and perhaps always has been considered as an element of the problem, but surely there are others that merit consideration. Mr. Justice Frankfurter would weigh all of them. Interstate commerce must pay its own way among the several states which give it protection, but the national market must not be sacrificed. Here again is the familiar clash of two rights, not right against wrong. "The incidence of the particular state enactment must determine whether it has transgressed the power left to the States to protect their special state interests although it is related to a phase of a more extensive commercial process."[54]

It has annoyed some that Mr. Justice Frankfurter, in striking a balance—or rather in judging the balance struck by others, has "reverted" to the old amorphous direct-burden language. It is characteristic that at least until something clearly better is found, he follows the old way. Of course, the "nine old men" perverted the "direct-burden" rule to their own "laissez-faire" purposes. Mr. Justice Frankfurter has not reverted to that usage; rather he has returned, if that term is applicable, to the approach that Mr. Justice Holmes expounded in the *Galveston Railway* case:

It appears sufficiently, perhaps from what has been said, that we are to look for a practical rather than a logical or philosophical distinction. The State must be allowed to tax the [railroad] property and to tax it at its actual value as a going concern. On the other hand the State cannot tax the interstate business. The two necessities hardly admit of an absolute logical reconciliation. Yet the distinction is not without sense.

When a legislature is trying simply to value property, it is less likely to attempt or effect injurious regulation than when it is aiming directly at the receipts from interstate commerce. A practical line can be drawn by taking the whole scheme of taxation into account. That must be done by this court as best it can. Neither the state courts nor the legislatures, by giving the tax a particular name or by use of some form of words, can take away our duty to consider its nature and effect. If it bears upon commerce among the States so directly as to amount to a regulation in a relatively immediate way, it will not be saved by name or form.[55]

It may be noted that Mr. Justice Brandeis, too, used the "direct-burden" rule.[56] Perhaps so many imponderables are involved in endless, ever changing *state and local* imposts as they impinge upon the nation that no more precise formula is possible. Surely it is significant that generations of judges struggling with the problem have not found one that is generally acceptable. What has been decisive, perhaps, are "the inexpressible insights of experience" in a situation too complex to be captured by any sharp rule. It is a commonplace that in this area the Court's results have been better than its ability to explain them.

If it be said that in view of his general hands-off attitude, Mr. Justice Frankfurter is rather free in rejecting state taxation of interstate commerce, the answer is clear. Such measures infringe upon the interests of persons outside the offending state. Texans who are damaged by a Louisiana tax cannot readily expect relief via the democratic processes in Louisiana;[57] and, as Mr. Justice Jackson pointed out, the damage will often not be extensive enough to attain the attention of Congress. Thus there is in these federalistic problems something of an hiatus, or interregnum, in the machinery of our democracy. Accordingly, the weight on the freedom-for-state-experimentation side of the scale is rather lighter than when a state affects only interests within the circle of its political processes. Moreover, Mr. Justice Frankfurter agrees fully with the Court that its decisions in this area—upholding or rejecting the state measures affecting interstate commerce—may be reversed by Congress, where all the people and all the states are represented.[58] It may be significant that the Justice refers to the Court's role in these cases as that of "mediator"—Chief Justice Stone used the term "arbiter." Such language in conjunction with the strange, not fully explained, power of Congress to override Court decisions as to the scope of state power under the Commerce Clause suggests that at least some judges conceive that in this area the Court acts in a nonjudicial capacity. Hence possibly the rather general avoidance of even relatively precise rules as being incompatible with the mediatory function.

A striking case is *Dean Milk Co.* v. *Madison.*[59] The county surrounding Madison, Wisconsin, had some 5,600 dairy farms supplying about ten times more milk than could be consumed locally. A municipal ordinance forbade the sale in Madison of milk not processed at an approved plant within five miles of the city. The Dean Milk Company, wanting to send Illinois milk into Madison, challenged the provision on Commerce Clause grounds. The Court, including Mr. Justice Frankfurter, held for the company:

> In thus erecting an economic barrier protecting a major local industry against competition from without the State, Madison plainly discriminates against interstate commerce. This it cannot do, even in the exercise of its unquestioned power to protect the health and safety of its people, if reasonable, non-discriminatory alternatives, adequate to conserve legitimate local interests, are available. . . . A different view, that the ordinance is valid simply because it professes to be a health measure would mean that the Commerce Clause of itself imposes no limitations on state action . . . save for the rare instance where a state artlessly discloses an avowed purpose to discriminate against interstate goods. Our issue then is whether the discrimination inherent in the Madison ordinance can be justified in view of the character of the local interests and the available methods of protecting them.
>
> It appears that reasonable and adequate alternatives are available.

Mr. Justice Black, joined by Douglas and Minton, dissented:

> This health regulation should not be invalidated merely be-
> cause the Court believes that alternative milk-inspection meth-
> ods might insure the cleanliness and healthfulness of Dean's
> Illinois milk. I find it difficult to explain why the Court uses
> the "reasonable alternative" concept to protect trade when
> today it refuses to apply the same principle to protect freedom
> of speech. *Feiner* v. *New York*, 340 U.S. 315. . . . Since the
> days of Chief Justice Marshall, federal courts have left states
> and municipalities free to pass bona fide health regulations
> subject only "to the paramount authority of Congress if it de-
> cides to assume control. . . ."

Obviously, one difference between the minority and majority
views is that where one saw only a health problem, the other
saw health plus economic discrimination. This is reminiscent
of *Dennis* and related cases where the dissenters saw only
speech, while a majority saw speech plus. Of course health and
free speech are crucial interests. But shall they override all
else? As in the *Steel Seizure* case a minor premise makes a
difference. Mr. Justice Frankfurter no doubt would agree with
Paul Freund that judicial values come "not in single file but
in battalions." Idealists, on the other hand, keep their eyes on
the ball. They are apt to isolate *one* element of a problem and
give it controlling status. What Philip Kurland said of two
judges no longer on the bench seems relevant here: ". . . neither
dealt with the cases presented as complex problems: for each
there was one issue which forced decision."

If, as suggested in Chapter 2, Mr. Justice Black tends to
focus on the needs of the specific case, as distinct from the
demands of legal principle, his *Dean Milk* and *Dennis* opinions
suggest that he is apt to concentrate not on the whole case but
on selected aspects of it. Indeed, he may, in the interests of
Justice, concentrate upon something strictly not before the
Court—as in *Terminiello*. Moreover, if need be, he can dis-
count facts as well as issues. Thus in his *Dean Milk* dissent the
Justice observes that the company could have its Illinois milk

pasteurized within five miles of Madison. "Therefore Dean's personal preference to pasteurize in Illinois, not the ordinance, keeps Dean's milk out of Madison." True enough, but to the company this must have sounded like Marie Antoinette's "Let them eat cake." Not caprice but business reality dictated the company's "personal preference" to pasteurize in Illinois. It had processing plants there; it had none within five miles of Madison.[60] Apparently on Mr. Justice Black's scale of values public health occupies a "preferred position" comparable to that of free discussion. More accurately, perhaps, it is simply that for him judicial (as distinct from congressional) protection for the national market ranks extremely low. Few, of course, will take without salt, as he did, the claim that the city of Madison was merely, or essentially, interested in health.

5 JUSTICE AND DEMOCRACY

> Congress and the President have all the force [sword and purse], if they dare use it, and the Court has nothing but its power to persuade us. . . .
>
> We too often forget that the reason for the great power of the Supreme Court is not that it interprets the Constitution to us, but that it reads our immanent patterns of behavior into our Constitution, and as it reads them into it, the Court explains them to us, and so makes us the more aware of them. And if it stresses the patterns of our better behavior, this is no more than the normative element in any good description.
>
> CHARLES P. CURTIS

SOMEWHERE in the Pacific Ocean lies an island untouched by the barbarities of modern culture. Life there is serene. Government is simple and above all successful. In the center of a crude stone temple rests the ancient skull of the community's founding father—attended by nine revered priests. When public issues cannot be settled by other means the priests consult the founder's skull. There they find the ultimate answers to all possible problems. If this is crude, it works. And it works because of the genius of the priests. Consciously, or unconsciously, what they "find" in the skull—or put there—is what they find in the conscience of community. The priesthood is not representative in any modern political sense. Superficially it might be called autocratic. Yet it has no force of arms and no control of the purse. Its only power is the power to persuade. Yet its persuasiveness is great because its pronouncements reflect not whim but slowly changing aspirations and felt needs of the community. The ancient symbol satisfies the humanly urgent need for stability. The priests provide the indispensable element of growth to meet changing social needs.

The myth of the skull no doubt will survive as long as the priesthood accurately reads and respects the emerging conscience of the community. Under such conditions the "consent of the governed" prevails. The ruled in fact rule. Were the priests to cling stubbornly to worn-out ideals they would soon be in trouble. So would they be if they insisted upon "progress" which the people were not yet prepared to accept. In either instance the "governed" would begin to see, and resent, that they were being ruled not by law (the skull) but by men.

Like the ancient skull, our Constitution does not provide answers to all possible social problems. Yet we expect the judges to find them there. Over the long run they have done an effective job. That is to say, their edicts have generally reflected the ever changing mores, or conscience, of the American people. At the height of the judicial crisis in 1936, Mr. Justice Stone posed the problem with the brevity of genius. The Constitution is largely open-ended. Where it speaks with less than precision the ultimate test is reason. But

> Whether the constitutional standard of reasonableness . . . is subjective, that of the judge who must decide, or objective in terms of a considered judgment of what the community may regard as within the limits of the reasonable, are questions which the cases have not specifically decided. Often these standards do not differ. When they do not, it is a happy augury for the development of law which is socially adequate. But the judge . . . must be ever alert to discover whether they do differ and, differing, whether his own or the objective standard will represent the sober second thought of the community, which is the firm base on which all law must ultimately rest.[1]

In stable times interpreting the community's basic sense of values is apt to be unconscious and automatic. But in eras of rapid social adjustment a judge's job approaches the impossible. The "nine old men" failed awesomely in the crisis of the

Great Depression. The Court's wound from that debacle had not fully healed when the Atomic Age and the cold war crisis were upon us.

A little learning is dangerous. Many discovered in the Court crisis of the 1930's that judges do not merely find, but sometimes make, the law. We came to see, as Max Lerner said, that judicial babies are not brought by constitutional storks. This secularization of the Court might have been all to the good, if we had also understood that lawmaking is an inherent and inevitable part of the judicial process. Judges, after all, must be more than mimics. Greatness on the bench, as elsewhere, is creativity. "We shall know," Cardozo said, "that the process of judging is a phase of a never ending movement, and that something more is expected of those who play their part in it than imitative reproduction, the lifeless repetition of a mechanical routine." Or, in the words of Curtis Bok, judging is "the play of an enlightened personality within the boundaries of a system." Of course judges sometimes make law. The great problem is how shall they contribute their bit to the law's growth without overstepping the boundaries of the system. Lord Bryce spoke of the need to reconcile tradition and convenience. Dean Pound referred to the competing claims of stability and change. Sir Frederick Pollock wrote brilliantly on judicial valor and caution.

> Obviously, the most abstruse and delicate piercings of modern mathematics or of chemistry could not achieve a formula for an appropriate apportionment of the relevant components of valor and caution, stability and change, tradition and convenience, in the myriad instances that solicit the judicial judgment.[2]

"That the courts," Frankfurter once bitterly observed, "are especially fitted to be the ultimate arbiters of policy is an intelligent and tenable doctrine. But let them and us face the fact that five Justices of the Supreme Court *are* conscious molders of policy instead of impersonal vehicles of revealed truth." The English apparently learned the lesson ages ago. They have long since reduced the judge's role to a minimum by rejecting judicial, in favor of parliamentary, supremacy. Either way, some human agency will have the "final" word. We give it to a Supreme Court, they give it to a supreme legislature. Assuming that we are to retain our system, the question is: how far and with what materials shall judges build the law? For build it they must.

Two great traditions provide two quite different approaches to these problems. One finds expression in Taney,[3] Waite, Holmes, Brandeis, Learned Hand, Stone, Cardozo, and Frankfurter. These are the humilitarians, the pragmatists. Recognizing that judicial legislation is inevitable, they would hold it to a minimum. Their attitude is strikingly revealed in the letters of Mr. Justice Stone and Professor Frankfurter. When Mr. Justice Black had been on the bench for only a few months his colleague Stone wrote Frankfurter:

> Do you know Black well? You might be able to render him great assistance. He needs guidance from someone who is more familiar with the workings of the judicial process than he is. . . . I am fearful though that he will not avoid the danger of frittering away his opportunity for judicial effectiveness by lack of good technique, and by the desire to express ideas which, however valuable they may be in themselves, are irrelevant or untimely. There are enough present-day battles of importance to be won without wasting our efforts to remake the Constitution *ab initio*, or using the judicial opinion as a political tract.[4]

This from the liberal Stone! Frankfurter's "assistance" to Mr. Justice Black is also instructive. Remember: at the time of this exchange in 1938 these three men were united in their opposition to the old judicial order. "Judges," Frankfurter wrote,

> cannot escape the responsibility of filling in gaps which the finitude of even the most imaginative legislation renders inevitable. And so it is that in the countries governed exclusively by codes and even in the best of all codes there are provisions saying in effect that when a controversy arises in court for for which the code offers no provision the judges are not relieved of the duty of deciding the case but must themselves fashion the law appropriate to the situation.

So the problem is not whether the judges make the law, but when and how much. Holmes put it in his highbrow way, that "they can do so only interstitially; they are confined from molar to molecular motions." I used to say to my students that legislatures make law wholesale, judges retail. In other words they cannot decide things by invoking a new major premise out of whole cloth; they must make the law that they do make out of the existing materials and with due reference to the presuppositions of the legal system of which they have been made a part. . . .

I think one of the evil features, a very evil one, about all this assumption that judges only find the law and don't make it, often becomes the evil of a lack of candor. By covering up the lawmaking function of judges, we miseducate the people and fail to bring out into the open the real responsibility of judges for what they do, leaving it to the primary lawmaking agency, the legislature, to correct what judges do if they don't like it, or to give them more specific directions than what they so often do by what is put on the statute books.[5]

The other tradition finds expression in Marshall, Field, Peckham, Fuller, Sutherland, and Black. These are the activists. For them judicial legislation is not incidental, it is the heart of the judicial process. They see great visions and feel compelled to embed them in the law. Or, more mildly, their creative impulses are guided by their ideals. One of Mr. Justice Black's ardent supporters put it this way: "As procedure is the instrument, not the master of law; so law is the instrument, not the master of justice." Law, then, is simply a tool to be manipulated in accordance with the judge's vision of right and wrong.

An old story has it that when Holmes departed to assume his duties on the Supreme Court he was admonished to do Justice. He responded thoughtfully that his job was merely to enforce the law. At best this little tale is incomplete, but it is significant. In an opinion that seems destined to live as long as the ideals of democracy survive, Justices Holmes and Brandeis rejected their colleagues' narrow conception of free speech, yet concurred in the judgment affirming conviction.[6] Though the accused had claimed protection under the appropriate constitutional provision, she had failed at the trial level to raise the "clear and present danger" issue. Raising it in the Supreme Court was futile, thought Holmes and Brandeis, because "Our power of review in this case is limited not only to the question whether a right guaranteed by the Federal Constitution was denied [in the state court] . . . but to the particular claims duly made below and denied." It may be said, of course, that Holmes and Brandeis had "no feel for the dominant issues"; that, pre-occupied with "crochet patches of legalism on the fingers of the case," they let a technicality prevail over Justice. Others may suppose the two great judges, well aware of what was at stake, deemed themselves not free to do Justice, but bound to do justice under law, i.e., in accordance with that very special allocation of function and authority which is the essence of Federalism and the Separation of Powers. The point is, one's estimate of a judge hangs on one's conception—articulate or otherwise—of the judicial function.

To those for whom the Supreme Court's first concern is Justice, a great judge on that bench is an activist, one who does not readily permit "technicalities" to frustrate the ultimate. It follows, of course, that in so far as activism prevails the Court is the final governing authority. For, to that extent, its basic job is to impose Justice upon all other agencies of government, in-deed upon the community itself. But what is Justice? Not so long ago, activists among the "nine old men" found it in a modified (read perverted) "laissez faire" called rugged indi-vidualism. Modern activists see it as a humane and virile liber-tarianism. Holmes facetiously suggested that its roots are in one's "can't helps."[7]

All this is unacceptable to those who take the more modest view that the Court's chief concern is *justice under law*. For them, the great judge is the humilitarian, the respecter of those "technicalities" which allocate among many agencies different responsibilities in the pursuit of Justice. In this view, the Court's special function is to preserve a constitutional balance between the several elements in a common enterprise. It maintains the ship, others set the course.

While these two views are distinct at their cores, they fuse into one another at their peripheries. Both are deep in American culture. Neither prevails to the complete exclusion of the other even in the work of a single judge. Eventually, the ardent activist gives way to a rule, just as his counterpart on occasion ignores rules for something deemed transcendental. What is important is the judge's inclination, his view of the nature of his role and the depth of his convictions.

Of the "great dissenters" in the days of "laissez-faire" activism only Harlan Stone remained on the bench to see the new libertarian activism after 1938. He was as unpersuaded by the one as by the other. In his view both entailed abuse of the judicial function. At the close of a long career spanning the two quite different eras of judicial Justice, he wrote a trusted friend,

> My more conservative brethren in the old days [read their preferences into legislation and] into the Constitution as well. What they did placed in jeopardy a great and useful institution of government. The pendulum has now swung to the other extreme, and history is repeating itself. The Court is now in as much danger of becoming a legislative and Constitution-making body, enacting into law its own predilections, as it was then.[8]

As Thomas Reed Powell put it, "Four of the Roosevelt appointees were as determined in *their* direction, as four of their predecessors were determined by attraction to the opposite pole."[9]

MR. JUSTICE BLACK'S ACTIVISM

Where Mr. Justice Sutherland gave a preferred place to dominant economic interests, Mr. Justice Black gives preference to the "underdog." Both positions spring from the same activist premise. Each finds in the law a special tenderness for a chosen (though different) set of values. Judicial idealism of this sort prospers if there is harmony between the judge's Justice and the prevailing ideals of the community. Disharmony brings disaster. The old Court rode high while "laissez faire" was in the air. It destroyed itself by clinging too long to moribund views. But anachronism may not be the most serious risk. Perhaps, in some eras—possibly today—there are no plainly dominant ideals. Maybe society is too perplexed, too pluralistic, too ridden with conflicting values to be captured meaningfully in any ideological common denominator. Moreover, there is always some discrepancy between thought and action. Sometimes the only function of an ideal is to appease the conscience, while institutions take more convenient forms.

Plainly, Mr. Justice Black leans one way when "liberal" values are at stake and another way in the face of "conservative" claims—be the issue one of constitutional law, statutory interpretation, or evaluation of evidence. This tendency no doubt is what critics have in mind when they charge the Court with judicial legislation. For, if at most one colleague goes the whole way with him, Mr. Justice Black is obviously a leader—perhaps the backbone—of the new Court's powerful, "liberal" wing. His humane sympathy for the common man, his courage, creative vigor, and perseverance mark him as a dedicated being in pursuit of utopian ends. But is the bench a proper vehicle to use in pursuing them?

Surely it is an idealized view of the American legislative and constitution-making process that finds the product inevitably favoring New Deal values. It was no less a fantasy, of course, for some of the "nine old men" to find the law so often favoring quite different interests. Activism, whether of the old or new variety, may be consistent with the legislator's function, but is it compatible with the basic judicial job of settling "cases" and "controversies" impartially?

Apologists for the modern version of activist Justice seem to concentrate upon its First Amendment aspects and ignore its economic implications as in the FELA, FLSA, ICC, NLRB, and Sherman Act cases. This permits them to rest upon—or hide behind—the hallowed generalities of democratic dogma. Even so, they do not argue that the Constitution guarantees absolute freedom of expression, or that any explicit limitation can be found in the written document. *Choice then is inevitable.* Yet we are not told why a legislative choice between competing interests here is, *a priori,* less worthy of respect than elsewhere. To put it differently, the activist position assumes that courts are somehow inherently more competent to achieve a sound balance of interests in First Amendment cases than in others.

Perhaps freedom of expression and religion are so overwhelmingly important that we must weight the scales of justice in their favor. But what of a judge who is also an activist in economic matters? Is there any point in free discussion if its legislative fruits—the accommodations of the democratic way of life—are to be undone by judicial fiat? Surely the free speech that produced the FLSA compromise, for example, was a waste of time, if all judges—like some—were to reject it for one of its extreme components. Ironically, those who are least respectful of a legislative balance of interests in speech cases are the very ones who show least respect for legislative compromise in the economic domain. A burning faith in democracy and impatience with its results is not a new quality among idealists.

Democracy does not contemplate vast governmental authority in hands that are free both of the legislator's political responsibility and the judge's checkrein of precedent. For a healthy society both stability and change are indispensable. Our separation of governmental functions imposes major responsibility for the one upon courts; for the other upon legislatures. If the judiciary is to be a free-wheeling, legislative body, it will inevitably forfeit "some of the credit needed to fulfill a role much more unique." For as Professor Jaffe suggests:[10]

> Our society *is* a class society, at the least a society of vigorously competing interests. It is also an exceedingly mobile so-

ciety, richly creating new opportunities, malignantly gener-
ating insecurities. It is a society which, in making unprece-
dented demands on government for change, places a heavy
strain on the agencies of stability. To compose the constantly
clashing demands for new opportunity our society sets up a
representative legislature. To compose the day-to-day differences between man and man, and between man and organized
society, it relies upon a nonrepresentative body of profession-
als. The warrant for their great power is the universal conviction that there is a knowable law which they can and will
apply by the exercise of reason. The faith in judicial objectivity is an ultimate source of personal security and social co-
hesion. But once it comes to be believed by one or another of
the great social classes that the Court is an organ of another
class, its function is impaired. This is peculiarly the case when
the Court is a constitutional one and participates in the very
creation of major social premises. To secure wholehearted and
widespread acceptance of its pronouncements it has need of
all the credit it can amass; to squander it on schemes for social
betterment is foolhardy.

In short there are special American reasons for the rejection
of Plato's "philosopher-king" in favor of Aristotle's Rule of
Law. If the latter is never fully attainable, if "reason" above
"personal preference" is an illusion, "to dispel it would cause
men to lose themselves in an even greater illusion: the illusion
that personal power can be benevolently exercised."[11]

Obviously, for Mr. Justice Black law is largely an instrument
in the service of his ideals. This leads him along two divergent
paths. Repelled by the "aberrations" of the old Court, he wants
certainty in the law. To this end he forges absolute rules. Initial-
ly they seem adequate to outlaw the old "mistakes" and to insure
achievement of his ideal Justice. But, just as constitutional and
legislative law cannot anticipate all concrete cases, neither can
Mr. Justice Black's "absolutes." Accordingly, in practice he is
as highhanded with his own, as with more orthodox, legal rules.
His zeal for certainty collides with his zeal for substantive
Justice. When this happens he is faced with raw personal
choice. Corporations (when they publish newspapers and are

involved in free press problems) suddenly and without explanation re-emerge as Fourteenth Amendment "persons," only to pass again into limbo. With due apology, the Commerce Clause regains its old power as a restraint upon the states (to block racial segregation). The Fourteenth Amendment ranges for a time beyond the standards enumerated in the Bill of Rights. Indeed, it has been known to acquire qualities that previously had been condemned as characteristic of "natural law."[12] Even the "preferred place" rule is riddled with gaps and quibbles. Thus, while Mr. Justice Black holds that evangelical peddling of religious tracts occupies "the same high estate" as worship in a church and so is immune from nondiscriminatory peddlers' taxes,[13] he does not find it immune from child labor regulations.[14] The latter holding was justified on the ground that the state has greater control over children than over adults. But we are not told why that greater control was not relevant in the second "flag salute" case.[15] Similarly, free speech via picketing gives way before a "liberal" antitrust law[16] but not before a "reactionary" right-to-work measure.[17] Juries are all important in FELA cases but count for little in certain others.

Mr. Justice Black is too sensible to follow wooden rules—including his own. But refusal to adhere to orthodox legal standards, as well as his own substitutes, leaves little but *ad hoc* grounds for decision. This freedom to attain the "just" result is presumably what John Frank meant when, with admiration, he wrote that Mr. Justice Black "sees the social point of a case, its implications to the lives of people, in a flash; and he has the energy and the ability to devise ways—new ways if need be— of serving what in his conception is the largest good. . . . His significance as a Justice is that he knows what to do with the power thus given him."[18]

Such creativity destroyed the old Court—and brought the associated state chief justices, among others, to condemn the new one for judicial legislation.[19] But Chief Justice Marshall, too, was condemned for "serving what in his conception [was] the largest good" in his day. To his admirers Hugo Black is another John Marshall: one who—before most of his contemporaries—saw and accommodated the needs of his age. Others see in him the shadow of Sutherland: a wilful judge who with honorable intent abused his power in pursuit of a mirage. Only time can render a true verdict. Meanwhile, men of generous instinct take heart in Hugo Black's bold stand.

Of course courts do not readily go beyond accepted norms of right and wrong; yet we cannot live forever in a moral status quo. Be it, or not, a judge's function, Mr. Justice Black's dissenting struggle in the realm of civil liberty challenges the conscience of the crowd. His restless probing at the frontiers of freedom may help us to achieve more enlightened notions of public decency—and thus inevitably a more enlightened legal order. In any case posterity may find it easier to understand his expansive views on civil liberty than his parochialism in economics—which is to say, posterity may not appreciate the lasting impact of the Great Depression and the New Deal upon a compassionate heart. In short, if the Justice errs, he errs on the side of a good Samaritan, a Samaritan marked by the peculiar economic problems of the early 1930's. With deep esteem born of close association John Frank has written:

> In deciding cases Black is frequently a sentimentalist about people. A vivid and dramatic imagination fills in details that may or may not exist. If a case involves an injured veteran, Black sees the veteran, and his family, and his children. If it should be an injured railroad worker, the man becomes as real to Black on an abstract record as if Black himself were making the address to the jury. In these and in the farmer foreclosure cases, now less frequent than they were, Black's sympathies are so completely and automatically enlisted for the unfortunate that he is very nearly as much of a pleader as a judge....
>
> At the same time Black is a very, very tough man. When he is convinced, he is cool steel hard. He knows clearly the kind of America he wants his children to grow up in, and he is absolutely impervious to blows that may fall upon him for trying to create that kind of America.[20]

Two things now seem clear: among the activists in our judicial history there are more Sutherlands than Marshalls; among those judges whom history has labeled "great," the humble outnumber the others.

Mr. Justice Frankfurter is deeply humilitarian. Plainly this is an acquired characteristic, a judicial mold superimposed upon a powerfully active and thoroughly libertarian personality. If to some his modesty seems exaggerated—breast-beating it has been called—that may be the measure of the struggle within him or within the Court. Just as Holmes was more skeptical, so he was less vocal in his humility. In any case, there can be no doubt of the deep Holmesian mark upon Mr. Justice Frankfurter. Before he took his seat upon the bench he was the intimate personal and professional confidant of Holmes, as well as Brandeis, during the whole, long course of their struggle against the activism of Sutherland and company. The shared ardors of that contest must have reinforced what Professor Frankfurter was learning as teacher of federal jurisdiction at Harvard; namely, that since the Supreme Court cannot review more than a drop in the flood of American litigation, by long established principle that drop must be selected, not on the basis of Justice to any litigant, but in the interest of balance among the various elements in the governmental structure. Moreover, if the Court takes jurisdiction on the one ground and decides on the other, balance is jeopardized and though Justice (in its then current version) be done for a few, the result is hardly fair to the many whose cases, however worthy, cannot for physical limitations hope to reach the judicial summit. What Paul Freund has said of Mr. Justice Brandeis is relevant here.

> [H]e would not be seduced by the quixotic temptation to right every fancied wrong which was paraded before him. The time was always out of joint but he was not [commissioned] to set it right. . . . Husbanding his time and energies as if the

next day were to be his last, he steeled himself, like a scientist in the service of man, against the enervating distraction of countless tragedies he was not meant to relieve. His concern for jurisdictional and procedural limits reflected, on the technical level, an essentially Stoic philosophy. For like Epictetus, he recognized "the impropriety of being emotionally affected by what is not under one's control."[21]

The basic articulate premise of government in the United States is the diffusion of power. Ultimate political control is spread broadly among the people. This is the foundation of democracy. Governmental power is divided between nation and states. This is Federalism. What is given to each is parceled out among three branches to accomplish the Separation of Powers. The purpose is not merely (as schoolboys emphasize) to avoid a tyrannical concentration of power. We seek, as well, the alignment of form to special function and, above all, that unique democratic efficiency, the promise that, if decisions be slow, they will be acceptable to those who must live with them.

For Mr. Justice Frankfurter, dispersion of the power to govern is not just a sophomoric slogan. It is the essence of our system. That is why he is so mindful of the political processes, state responsibility and the division of labor between legislative, executive, administrative, and judicial agencies. In Professor Jaffe's thoughtful account, the Justice is "forever disposing of issues by assigning their disposition to some other sphere of competence."

But this is only half the problem. Familiarity obscures for us what to outsiders is a marked characteristic of American government: our habit of dressing up the most intricate social, economic, and political problems in legal jargon and presenting them to the courts for "adjudication." In view of this, a foreign observer long ago concluded that, if asked where he found the American aristocracy, i.e., the governing class, he would reply "without hesitation . . . that it occupies the judicial bench and bar." Perhaps the short of it is that behind and overshadowing our open commitment to the fragmentation of power lies a brooding, inarticulate distrust of popular government. This finds expression in judicial review, or judicial supremacy. Whatever the name, the essence is clear: *concentration in a single agency*—significantly, that farthest removed from the people—of power to override all other elements of government, whether at the national, state, or local level. Neither Congress nor the President, no administrative agency, no governor, no state court or legislature, not a single city or county functionary is immune from the centralized power of judicial review. Indeed, in some eras the Court has been so domineering—in the name of Justice—that from time to time dissenters have felt compelled to remind it that the judiciary is "not the only agency of government that must be assumed to have capacity to govern." Equally pointed reminders have come from the outside. Most of the great leaders of American democracy, Jefferson, Jackson, Lincoln, Bryan, and the two Roosevelts, among others, have challenged the practice of judicial review. But, except perhaps in some academic circles, the principle has withstood abuse and criticism. It stands only a shade less firmly grounded in our polity than its counterpart, the dispersion of power.

The Supreme Court, then, is caught between basic principles that look in different directions. Mr. Justice Frankfurter seems more sensitive to the pinch than most, though doubtless no one in his position is immune. What is the judge's role in such an impasse? A common "compromise" has been to emphasize diffusion of power or judicial supremacy according to the nature of the interest before the Court. At least since the Civil War some judges have demonstrated a marked propensity to assert their supremacy for the benefit of "private property," while others have shown a tendency to distrust the principle of diffusion only when "personal liberty" is at issue. For Mr. Justice Frankfurter such compromises only underscore the lawless quality of the Court's power. Deeply libertarian in private thought and action, he sees what partisans do not see: that if effective transcendental arguments may be made for the social priority of personal liberty, no less powerful considerations in the abstract would sustain the primacy of economic interests. What Wilmon Sheldon said of philosophers seems relevant to those who hold to either extreme. They are generally right in what they affirm of their own vision and generally wrong in what they deny in the vision of others. There is more subtlety, more depth, and more complexity in our culture than such one-sided polemics dream of. We may be proud of the golden thread of liberalism that runs through American thought, but it is futile to pretend that the "acquisitive instinct" and the old Whiggish concern for property are not as deep in our culture. As Daniel Webster put it long ago, "Life and personal liberty are, no doubt, to be protected by law; but property is also to be protected by law, and is the fund out of which the means for protecting life and liberty are usually furnished." President Hadley of Yale spoke for many when he explained the Constitution as a "set of limitations on the political power of the majority in favor of the political power of the property owner." Such suggestions of the primacy of economic interests are wormwood to libertarians, but the disease is deep. Man must eat and, not less important, he must "know where his next meal is coming from." Our cold war experience in the "backward" areas of the world suggests that those who must choose are far more interested in economic security than in civil liberty. In any event it is important that neither is fungible and neither in the abstract is ever at stake in litigation. Typically, some finite facet of one or both is imperiled, and certainly in the kind of cases that now reach the Supreme Court the context is often such that intelligent men may differ as to whether a legitimate interest or its abuse is involved. This is what Holmes meant when he said that "general propositions do not decide concrete cases." Or, in Mr. Justice Cardozo's words, "Many an appeal to freedom is the masquerade of privilege or inequality seeking to entrench itself behind the catchword of a principle." For the purpose of settling specific litigation abstract arguments as to the relative importance of personal as against proprietary interests are as futile as medieval arguments about realism and nominalism. They cut no wood. Morris Cohen has called "attention to the fact that the traditional dilemmas, on which people have for a long time taken opposite stands, generally rest on difficulties rather than real contradictions, and that positive gains . . . can be made not by simply trying to prove that one side or the other is the truth, but by trying to get at the difficulty and determining in what respect and to what extent each side is justified."[22] This principle of polarity is the foundation of Mr. Justice Frankfurter's jurisprudence. He cannot be true to the American tradition and ignore the diffusion of power or judicial supremacy. Least of all can he accept reconciliation which raises now one and then another cluster of interests to a "preferred position" and correspondingly defers others.

Despite unqualified language in some parts of the Bill of Rights, no past or present member of the Court has even suggested that its liberties are unlimited. As with the "rights of property," the basic question always has been how and where to locate boundaries. Brandeis taught us anew, when we were in danger of forgetting it, that law is born of fact. "*Ex facto jus oritur*. That ancient rule must prevail in order that we may have a system of living law." The facts, after all, make up the issue. The precise problem of a minimum wage case,[23] for example, is evaded, not solved, by invoking the abstraction "liberty of contract," just as the *Terminiello* case is not solved by "reiterating generalized approbations of freedom of speech." A Brandeis concern for facts is as relevant in the one situation as in the other, if the Court is to decide real, not hypothetical, cases. It follows for Mr. Justice Frankfurter that judicial intrusion upon governmental policy is permissible only when the special facts of a concrete case leave no room for doubt. Since uncertainty entails choice, constitutional doubt must be resolved in favor of the views of those to whom primary governing authority has been given—and the people to whom they must answer.

This maxim of judicial self-restraint is not limited to constitutional law. It finds expression also in Mr. Justice Frankfurter's doctrine of "expertise" in the administrative law cases; in his willingness to accept legislative compromise—however uninspired—in the statutory interpretation cases; in his constant efforts to prevent federal, judge-made law from intruding upon local management of local affairs; and in his insistence in the *certiorari* cases that the Supreme Court stick to its limited and very special business. In the eyes of one critic, this demonstrates that "Mr. Justice Frankfurter has no feel for the dominant isues; he operates best when weaving crochet patches of legalism on the fingers of the case . . . it is a calamity that his skills happen to be petty skills."[24] Another has written that "the ex-professor . . . remained a rather narrow academician, engrossed in the trivia of formal legal propriety . . . to the disregard of the tough stuff of judicial statesmanship."[25] Obviously these critics are ardent supporters of Mr. Justice Black. It is ironical that the very characteristic which won for Felix Frankfurter an appointment to the bench—his insistence that the "dominant issues," i.e., policy-making, should be left to the democratic process—is now considered a vice by his critics. Obviously they like extensive judicial legislation, provided it is of the "new" libertarian, rather than the old, proprietarian, variety. To put it crudely, much depends upon whose ox is being gored or whose ideals are at stake.

If, as tradition holds, the law is a jealous mistress, it also has the feminine capacity to tempt each devotee to find his own image in her bosom. No one escapes entirely. Some yield blindly, some with sophistication. A few more or less effectively resist—Cardozo, because he could not quite forget that ethic of self-denial which man has never mastered; Holmes, from the hopeful scepticism of an inquiring mind; Frankfurter, largely, perhaps, from remembrance of things past. Surely wilfulness on the bench prior to 1937 was a catalyst in the making of all the "Roosevelt judges." Some of them with appropriate apologetics seemed to fly to an opposite wilfulness. Mr. Justice

Frankfurter has tried to subsume will to law and, where the law is vague, judicial will to the will, or conscience, of the community. If he falters, is it that his grasp is short, or that his reach is long? The discrepancy, a poet tells us, is "what a heaven's for." Meanwhile, such a judge must carry a heavier burden than does he whose commitment to proprietarian or libertarian abstractions—whose sense of Justice—is automatically decisive. "Believing it still important to do so," Mr. Justice Frankfurter has

> tried to dispel the age-old illusion that the conflicts to which the energy and ambition and imagination of the restless human spirit give rise can be subdued ... by giving the endeavors of reason we call law a mechanical or automatic or enduring configuration. Law cannot be confined within any such mold because life cannot be so confined.[26]

The Justice has lived too long with legal problems to be fooled by the simple antinomy. Abraham Lincoln made the point when he cut short the ranting of a northern extremist, "Mr. ———, haven't you lived long enough to know that two men may honestly differ about a question and both be right?" In this paradox lies the genius of our system.

> Often "the American Way of Life" is pictured in terms of rigid adherence to some idealogy, ignoring that our search for "a more perfect union" has been directed less to seeking final solutions than at establishing a tolerable balance of conflict among ourselves.[27]

Tolstoi saw that a great leader never leads. Does a great judge? At least for cases that reach the Supreme Court the law is seldom clear. The typical controversy entails a clash of interests, each of which has some, but no plainly preponderant, legal foundation. Yet the Court is expected to give a decision. And so perhaps in the end the intrinsic problem is this: for whom or in what direction shall doubt be resolved? Some have made uncertainty the servant of selected business interests. Others have been guided by more generous considerations. In Mr. Justice Frankfurter's view this "sovereign prerogative of choice" is not for judges. He would resolve all reasonable doubt in favor of the integrity of sister organs of government and the people to whom they must answer. He would adhere, that is, to the deepest of all our constitutional traditions, the dispersion of power—though, as in the "flag salute" cases, the immediate result offend his own generous heart's desire. He is wary of judicial attempts to impose Justice on the community; to deprive it of the wisdom that comes from self-inflicted wounds and the strength that grows with the burden of responsibility. It is his deepest conviction that no five men, or nine, are wise enough or good enough to wield such power over the lives of millions. In his view, humanitarian ends are served best in that allocation of function through which the people by a balance of power seek their own destiny. True to the faith upon which democracy ultimately rests, the Justice would leave to the political processes the onus of building legal standards in the vacuum of doubt. For in his view only that people is free who chooses for itself when choice must be made.

Epilogue—1966

*T*HOSE who praise, as well as those who criticize, Mr. Justice Black agree in general that he has been an inspired activist. As one of his admirers put it recently: "The active court is the indispensable means for the preservation of a vital constitution capable of *adapting itself* to the changes in society. Its activeness is not opposed to law. Indeed no other kind of court can maintain the law's meaning. The active court is the keystone of Black's philosophy. . . ."[1]

On June 4, 1964 (a few months after that paragraph was published), Mr. Justice Black found himself on the anti-activist, "illiberal" side of a constitutional issue involving the racial "sit-in."[2] Indeed his position favored "property" over "personal" interests; a "literal" versus an imaginative interpretation of the Fourteenth Amendment; the Harlan-White over the Warren-Douglas-Goldberg wing of the Court. A year later in opinions by Justices Douglas and Goldberg the Constitution "adapted itself" by recognizing a new right to privacy "emanating from" specific guarantees in the Bill of Rights.[3] Again Mr. Justice Black dissented—this time rejecting not merely a particular liberal and activist judgment, but activism itself:

> I realize that many good and able men have eloquently spoken and written, sometimes in rhapsodical strains, about the duty of this Court to keep the Constitution in tune with the times. The idea is that the Constitution must be changed from time to time and that this Court is charged with a duty to make those changes. For myself, I must with all deference

reject that philosophy. The Constitution makers knew the need for change and provided for it. Amendments suggested by the people's elected representatives can be submitted to the people or their selected agents for ratification. That method of change was good for our Fathers, and being somewhat old-fashioned I must add it is good enough for me. And so, I cannot rely on the Due Process Clause or the Ninth Amendment or any mysterious and uncertain natural law concept as a reason for striking down this state law. The Due Process Clause with an "arbitrary and capricious" or "shocking to the conscience" formula was liberally used by this Court to strike down economic legislation in the early decades of this century, threatening, many people thought, the tranquility and stability of the Nation. See, e.g., Lochner v. State of New York, 198 U.S. 45. . . . That formula, based on subjective considerations of "natural justice," is no less dangerous when used to enforce this Court's views about personal rights than those about economic rights. I had thought that we had laid that formula, as a means for striking down state legislation, to rest once and for all in cases like West Coast Hotel Co. v. Parrish, 300 U.S. 379, . . . Olsen v. State of Nebraska ex rel. Western Reference & Bond Assn., 313 U.S. 236, . . . and many other opinions. . . .

. . . And only six weeks ago, without even bothering to hear argument, this Court overruled Tyson & Brother v. Banton, 273 U.S. 418, . . . which had held state laws regulating ticket brokers to be a denial of due process of law. Gold v. DiCarlo, 380 U.S. ——, 85 S.Ct. 1332. I find April's holding hard to square with what my concurring Brethren urge today. They would reinstate the Lochner, Coppage, Adkins, Burns line of cases, cases from which this Court recoiled after the 1930's, and which had been I thought totally discredited until now. Apparently my Brethren have less quarrel with state economic regulations than former Justices of their persuasion had. But any limitation upon their using the natural law due process philosophy to strike down any state law, dealing with any activity whatever, will obviously be only self-imposed. . . .

. . . The late Judge Learned Hand, after emphasizing his view that judges should not use the due process formula suggested in the concurring opinions today or any other formula like it to invalidate legislation offensive to their "personal preferences," made the statements, with which I fully agree, that:

"For myself it would be most irksome to be ruled by a bevy of Platonic Guardians, even if I knew how to choose them, which I assuredly do not."

So far as I am concerned, Connecticut's law as applied here is not forbidden by any provision of the Federal Constitution as that Constitution was written, and I would therefore affirm.[4]

Perhaps under the impact of his brother Goldberg's ultra-activism, Mr. Justice Black has changed his mind about the role of courts in a democracy. Perhaps, finding that the Court has gone too far, he now accepts the "old-fashioned" Holmes-Hand-Frankfurter view that keeping law abreast of life is primarily a legislative, not a judicial, function. Or is he convinced that—whatever friends and foes may think—he has always been an anti-activist, adhering to the plain mandates of the written law?[5]

Notes and References

CHAPTER 1

The Depression, Hitler, and the Law

1. The classic example is *Hammer* v. *Dagenhart*, 247 U.S. 251 (1918).
2. The classic example is *Lochner* v. *New York*, 198 U.S. 45 (1905).
3. *In re Debs*, 158, U.S. 564 (1895).
4. For examples see cases referred to in notes 1 and 2, above.
5. *The Social Circle Case*, 162 U.S. 184 (1896); *Maximum Rate Case*, 167 U.S. 479 (1897); *ICC* v. *Alabama Midland Ry.*, 168 U.S. 144 (1897); *Wabash, St. Louis and Pacific Ry.* v. *Illinois*, 118 U.S. 557 (1886).
6. *U.S.* v. *E. C. Knight*, 156 U.S. 1 (1895).
7. *Pollock* v. *Farmers' Loan and Trust Co.*, 158 U.S. 601 (1895).
8. Quoted in Ralph Gabriel, *The Course of American Democratic Thought* (New York: Ronald Press Co., 1956), p. 163.
9. See Brookings Institution, *America's Capacity to Produce*, and *America's Capacity to Consume*. (1934).
10. For example, the Agricultural Adjustment Act, the National Labor Relations Act, the Fair Labor Standards Act, and the Social Security Act were calculated to improve the purchasing power of the farmer, of labor, and of the aged and handicapped. The Reciprocal Trade Agreements Act was designed to restore foreign trade.
11. 9 University of Chicago Law Review 393 (1942).
12. See, for example, *Gibbons* v. *Ogden*, 9 Wheaton 1 (1924).
13. See, for example, *Munn* v. *Illinois*, 94 U.S. 113 (1877).

CHAPTER 2

The Separation of Powers

1. *Youngstown Sheet & Tube Co.* v. *Sawyer*, 343 U.S. 579 (1952).
2. Reproduced in Irving Dilliard, *The Spirit of Liberty* (New York: Alfred A. Knopf, 1952), p. 109. Cf. the rule in *Heydon's Case*, 75 Eng. Rep. 637 (1584).

3. Felix Frankfurter, "Some Reflections on the Reading of Statutes," 47 Columbia Law Review 527, 528 (1947).

4. Thomas V. Smith, *The Legislative Way of Life* (Chicago: University of Chicago Press, 1940), p. 91.

5. Reproduced in Dilliard, *op. cit.*, pp. 173–74.

6. See John S. Forsyth, "Legislative History of the Fair Labor Standards Act," 6 Law & Contemporary Problems 464 (1939). The Commerce Clause will be found in Article I, sec. 10, of the Constitution.

7. *Ibid.*

8. *Kirshbaum* v. *Walling*, 316 U.S. 517 (1942).

9. *Borden Co.* v. *Borella*, 325 U.S. 679 (1945), Stone and Roberts dissenting.

10. *10 East 40th St. Bldg.* v. *Callus*, 325 U.S. 578 (1945).

11. The dissent in *Borden* would cover *Callus*. See the concurring opinion of the Chief Justice in the latter.

12. 335 U.S. 377 (1948).

13. *Western Union* v. *Lenroot*, 323 U.S. 490 (1945).

14. When Congress later reconsidered the child labor problem in 1949 it reversed itself (not the Court) by adopting a rather comprehensive prohibition similar to the one it had rejected in the Senate bill of 1937.

15. *McLeod* v. *Threlkeld*, 319 U.S. 491 (1943).

16. In *Farmer's Irrigation Co.* v. *McComb*, 337 U.S. 755 (1949), the issue was whether employees of a farmers' mutual irrigation company supplying water for the production of crops for interstate distribution were engaged "in any process or occupation necessary to the production" of goods for commerce, or, on the other hand, were "employed in agriculture" and so exempt from FLSA. A divided Court found the act applicable. In a brief concurring opinion, Mr. Justice Frankfurter observed that the case "presents a problem for construction which may with nearly equal reason be resolved one way rather than another. . . . The nature of the problem being what it is, I acquiesce in the judgment that commends itself to the majority of my brethren." In other words, in a "toss-up" case the Justice, obviously unsure of what Congress had meant, and without any established industrial tradition for a guide, followed the act's administrator and the Court in a liberal view. Here, along with Mr. Justice Black, he was "reversed" by act of Congress. The unanimous decisions in *Martino* v. *Michigan Window Cleaning Co.*, 327 U.S. 173 (1946), and *Roland Electric Co.* v. *Walling*, 326 U.S. 657 (1946), were "reversed" by act of Congress in 1949.

17. Sec. 7(a) (3), 29 U.S.C. Sec. 207 (1952).

18. *Bay Ridge Operating Co.* v. *Aaron*, 334 U.S. 446 (1948).

19. *Anderson* v. *Mt. Clemens Pottery Co.*, 328 U.S. 680 (1946); *Jewell Ridge Corp.* v. *Local No. 6167, UAW*, 325 U.S. 161 (1945).

20. *Schulte Co.* v. *Gangi*, 328 U.S. 108 (1946).

21. *Mitchell* v. *Kentucky Finance Co.*, 359 U.S. 290 (1959) ; *Mitchell* v. *Lublin, McGaughy & Assocs.*, 358 U.S. 207 (1959) ; *Mitchell* v. *Budd*, 350 U.S. 473 (1956) ; *Mitchell* v. *King Packing Co.*, 350 U.S. 260 (1956) ; *Steiner* v. *Mitchell*, 350 U.S. 247 (1956) ; *Mitchell* v. *Vollmer Co.*, 349 U.S. 427 (1955) ; *Maneja* v. *Waialua Agricultural Co.*, 349 U.S. 254 (1955) ; *Thomas* v. *Hempt Bros.*, 345 U.S. 19 (1953) ; *Alstate Const. Co.* v. *Durkin*, 345 U.S. 13 (1953) ; *Powell* v. *United States Cartridge Co.*, 339 U.S. 497 (1950) ; *Farmers Reservoir & Irrigation Co.*, v. *McComb*, 337 U.S. 755 (1949) ; *Vermilyn-Brown* v. *Connell*, 335 U.S. 377 (1949) ; *Bay Ridge Operating Co.* v. *Aaron*, 334 U.S. 446 (1958) ; *Morris* v. *McComb*, 332 U.S. 422 (1947) ; *Rutherford Food Corp.* v. *McComb*, 331 U.S. 722 (1947) ; *149 Madison Ave. Corp.* v. *Asselta*, 331 U.S. 199 (1947) ; *Walling* v. *Halliburton Oil Well Cementing Co.*, 331 U.S. 17 (1947) ; *Levinson* v. *Spector Motor Service*, 330 U.S. 649 (1947) ; *Walling* v. *General Industries Co.*, 330 U.S. 545 (1947) ; *Walling* v. *Nashville, C. & St. L. Ry.*, 330 U.S. 158 (1947) ; *Walling* v. *Portland Terminal Co.*, 330 U.S. 148 (1947) ; *Anderson* v. *Mt. Clemens Pottery Co.*, 328 U.S. 680 (1946) ; *D. A. Schulte* v. *Gangi*, 328 U.S. 108 (1946) ; *Boutell* v. *Walling*, 327 U.S. 463 (1946) ; *Mabee* v. *White Plains Pub. Co.*, 327 U.S. 178 (1946) ; *Oklahoma Press Pub. Co.* v. *Walling*, 327 U.S. 186 (1946) ; *Martino* v. *Michigan Window Cleaning Co.*, 327 U.S. 173 (1946) ; *Roland Elec. Co.* v. *Walling*, 326 U.S. 657 (1946) ; *Borden Co.* v. *Borella*, 325 U.S. 679 (1945) ; *10 East 40th St. Bldg.* v. *Callus*, 325 U.S. 578 (1945) ; *Walling* v. *Harnischfeger Corp.*, 325 U.S. 427 (1945) ; *Walling* v. *Youngerman-Reynolds*, 325 U.S. 419 (1945) ; *Jewell Ridge Coal Corp.* v. *Local No. 6167*, 325 U.S. 161 (1945) ; *J. F. Fitzgerald Const. Co.* v. *Pedersen*, 324 U.S. 720 (1945) ; *Brooklyn Sav. Bank* v. *O'Neil*, 324 U.S. 697 (1945) ; *A. H. Phillips, Inc.* v. *Walling*, 324 U.S. 490 (1945) ; *Gemsco* v. *Walling*, 324 U.S. 244 (1945) ; *Western Union* v. *Lenroot*, 323 U.S. 490 (1945) ; *United States* v. *Rosenwasser*, 323 U.S. 360 (1945) ; *Skidmore* v. *Swift & Co.*, 323 U.S. 134 (1944) ; *Armour & Co.* v. *Wantock*, 323 U.S. 126 (1944) ; *Walling* v. *Helmerich-Payne*, 323 U.S. 37 (1944) ; *Addison* v. *Holly Hill Fruit Co.*, 322 U.S. 607 (1944) ; *Walling* v. *Reuter, Inc.*, 321 U.S. 671 (1944) ; *Tennessee Coal, Iron & R. Co.* v. *Muscoda Local No. 123*, 321 U.S. 590 (1944) ; *Walton* v. *Southern Package Corp.*, 320 U.S. 540 (1944) ; *McLeod* v. *Threlkeld*, 319 U.S. 491 (1943) ; *Southland Gasoline Co.* v. *Bayley*, 319 U.S. 44 (1943) ; *Overstreet* v. *North Shore Corp.*, 318 U.S. 125 (1943) ; *Higgins* v. *Carr Bros. Co.*, 317 U.S. 572 (1943) ; *Walling* v. *Jacksonville Paper Co.*, 317 U.S. 564 (1943) ; *Warren-Bradshaw Drilling Co.*, v. *Hall*, 317 U.S. 88 (1942) ; *Walling* v. *Belo Corp.*, 316 U.S. 624 (1942) ; *Overnight Motor Transp. Co.* v. *Missel*, 316 U.S. 572 (1942) ; *Kirshbaum* v. *Walling*, 316 U.S. 517 (1942) ; *Cudahay* v. *Holland*, 315 U.S. 357 (1942) ; *Williams* v. *Jacksonville Terminal Co.*, 315 U.S. 386 (1942) ; *Opp Cotton Mills* v.

Administrator, 312 U.S. 126 (1941); *United States* v. *Darby*, 312 U.S. 100 (1941).

22. *Walling* v. *Nashville, C. & St. L. Ry.*, 330 U.S. 158 (1947); *Walling* v. *Portland Terminal Co.*, 330 U.S. 148 (1947); *Southland Gasoline Co.* v. *Bayley*, 319 U.S. 44 (1943); *Higgins* v. *Carr Bros.*, 317 U.S. 572 (1943). Cf. *Walling* v. *Jacksonville Paper Co.*, 317 U.S. 564 (1943).

23. The American Bar Association and the United States Railroad Retirement Board have urged replacement of FELA by a workmen's compensation system. See Alfred Conrad, "Workmen's Compensation: Is It More Efficient Than Employer's Liability?" 38 American Bar Association Journal 1011–14 (1952).

24. Senate Report No. 711, 75th Cong., 1st sess., 39 (1937).

25. See Henry Hart, "Foreword: The Time Chart of the Justices," 73 Harvard Law Review 84 (1959).

26. *Wilkerson* v. *McCarthy*, 336 U.S. 53 (1949).

27. The cases through February 25, 1957, are listed in Appendix B to the opinion of Mr. Justice Frankfurter in *Rogers* v. *Missouri Pacific Rd.*, 352 U.S. 500, 518, 549–59 (1957). The later cases are listed in the appendix to Mr. Justice Douglas' opinion in *Harris* v. *Pennsylvania Rd.*, 80 S.Ct. 22, 25–29 (1959).

28. *Herdman* v. *Pennsylvania Rd.*, 352 U.S. 518 (1957).

29. Between the demise of Justices Murphy and Rutledge and the advent of Chief Justice Warren there was a substantial lull in FELA cases in the Supreme Court.

30. See, for example, Mr. Justice Harlan's views in *Rogers* v. *Mo. Pacific Rd.*, 352 U.S. 500, 559 (1957).

31. *Griswold* v. *Gardner*, 155 Fed. (2d) 333 (7th Cir. 1946).

32. It may be worth notice that under the old judicial regime *certiorari* in FELA cases had a marked tendency to favor employers. Thus in ten Terms (1923–32) the Court reached an antilabor result on evidentiary grounds in twenty-nine out of thirty-five cases in which *certiorari* had been granted. See *Rogers* v. *Missouri Pacific Rd.*, 352 U.S. 518, 524, 542 (1957).

33. 350 U.S. 898 (1955).

34. 351 U.S. 183 (1956).

35. 79 S.Ct. 2 (1958).

36. See *Rogers* v. *Missouri Pacific Rd.*, 352 U.S. 500, 509 (1957).

37. *Herdman* v. *Pennsylvania Rd.*, 352 U.S. 518 (1957).

37a. For an example of how Supreme Court review could be expanded in the name of trial by jury, see the apparently stillborn effort in *Dick* v. *New York Life Insurance Company*, 359 U.S. 437 (1959).

38. See Mr. Justice Black's position in *Yates* v. *United States*, 354 U.S. 298 (1957); *Keegan* v. *United States*, 325 U.S. 478 (1945); *Hartzel* v. *United States*, 322 U.S. 680 (1944); *Ashcraft* v. *Tennessee*, 322

U.S. 143 (1944) ; *Lisenba* v. *California*, 314 U.S. 219 (1941).

38a. See, for example, the line of cases beginning with *Mahnich* v. *Southern S.S. Co.*, 321 U.S. 96 (1944) where the "liberal" position is that regardless of fault the employer is absolutely liable to seamen and some others for injuries growing out of "unseaworthiness." As to trial by jury in admiralty cases see dissent in *Crumady* v. *The Joachim Hendrick Fisser*, 358 U.S. 423 at 429 (1959).

39. *Phillips Petroleum Co.* v. *Oklahoma*, 340 U.S. 190, 192 (1950) ; *Cities Service Gas Co.* v. *Peerless Oil and Gas Co.*, 340 U.S. 179, 189 (1950) ; *International Shoe Co.* v. *Washington*, 326 U.S. 310, 322 (1945). See also *Polk Co.* v. *Glover*, 305 U.S. 5, 10 (1938).

40. *Klors Inc.* v. *Broadway-Hale*, 359 U.S. 207 (1959) ; *International Boxing Club* v. *United States*, 358 U.S. 242 (1959) ; *Northern Pacific Ry.* v. *United States*, 356 U.S. 1 (1958) ; *United States* v. *E. I. Du Pont De Nemours*, 353 U.S. 586 (1957) ; *United States* v. *E. I. Du Pont De Nemours*, 351 U.S. 377 (1956) ; *United States* v. *McKesson & Robbins*, 351 U.S. 305 (1956) ; *Theatre Enterprises* v. *Paramount Film Co.*, 346 U.S. 537 (1954) ; *Times-Picayune Publishing Co.* v. *United States*, 345 U.S. 594 (1953) ; *FTC* v. *Motion Picture Advertising Co.*, 344 U.S. 392 (1953) ; *Besser Mfg. Co.* v. *United States*, 343 U.S. 444 (1952) ; *United States* v. *Oregon Medical Ass'n.*, 342 U.S. 326 (1952) ; *United States* v. *New Wrinkle*, 342 U.S. 371 (1952) ; *Lorain Journal v. United States*, 342 U.S. 143 (1951) ; *Timken Roller Bearing Co.* v. *United States*, 341 U.S. 593 (1951) ; *Emich Motors* v. *General Motors*, 340 U.S. 558 (1951) ; *Keefer -Stewart* v. *Jos. E. Seagram Co.*, 340 U.S. 211 (1951) ; *United States* v. *United States Gypsum*, 340 U.S. 76 (1951) ; *United States* v. *National Real Estate Bds.*, 339 U.S. 485 (1950) ; *United States* v. *Yellow Cab*, 338 U.S. 338 (1949).

41. 328 U.S. 61 (1946).

42. *Cleveland* v. *United States*, 329 U.S. 14 (1946).

43. *Reider* v. *Thompson*, 339 U.S. 113 (1950).

44. *Scott Paper Co.* v. *Marcalus Co.*, 326 U.S. 249 (1954).

45. *Mahnich* v. *Southern S.S. Co.*, 321 U.S. 96 (1944).

46. *Tiller* v. *Atlantic Coast Line Rd.*, 318 U.S. 54 (1943).

47. *United States* v. *I.C.C.*, 337 U.S. 426 (1949).

48. *Mahnich* v. *Southern S.S. Co.*, 321 U.S. 96, 113 (1944). In *Helvering* v. *Hallock*, 309 U.S. 106 (1944), and *Rochester Telephone Co.* v. *United States*, 307 U.S. 125 (1939), for example, Mr. Justice Frankfurter apparently found precedents so confusing, if not contradictory, as to justify reversal.

49. 322 U.S. 533 (1944).

50. The first case in this line simply held that "issuing a policy of insurance is not a transaction of commerce." *Paul* v. *Virginia*, 8 Wallace 168, 183 (1869). The broader language quoted above appeared in *Hooper* v. *California*, 155 U.S. 648, 654–55 (1895).

51. 318 U.S. 371 (1943).

52. *Eisner* v. *Macomber*, 252 U.S. 189 (1920).

53. *Koshland* v. *Helvering*, 298 U.S. 441 (1936).

54. 312 U.S. 219 (1941).

55. 254 U.S. 443 (1921).

56. Quoted in the *Hutcheson* case at p. 236.

57. A discussion of the NLRB cases will be found immediately below.

58. Frankfurter concurring in *Driscoll* v. *Edison Light & Power Co.*, 307 U.S. 104, 122 (1939).

59. *United States* v. *Morgan*, 313 U.S. 409, 422 (1941).

60. *Administrative Justice and the Supremacy of the Law* (Cambridge, Mass.: Harvard University Press, 1927), p. 55.

61. E. Merick Dodd, "The Supreme Court and Organized Labor, 1941–1945," 58 Harvard Law Review 1018, 1066–67 (1945). During the period in question the Labor Board was notably "liberal," while the ICC was quite conservative. See Huntington, "The Marasmus of the ICC," 61 Yale Law Journal 476 (1952).

62. The cases are listed in Dodd, *loc. cit.*, p. 1067.

63. *Pan-Atlantic Steamship Corp.* v. *Atlantic Coastline R. Co.*, 353 U.S. 476 (1957) ; *Allegheny Corp.* v. *Breswick Co.*, 353 U.S. 151 (1957) ; *United States* v. *ICC*, 352 U.S. 158 (1956) ; *Denver & Rio Grande Rd.* v. *Union Pacific Rd.*, 351 U.S. 321 (1956) ; *Dixie Carriers* v. *United States*, 351 U.S. 56 (1956) ; *East Texas Motor Freight* v. *Frozen Food Exp.*, 351 U.S. 49 (1956) ; *United States* v. *Contract Steel Carriers*, 350 U.S. 409 (1956) ; *Secretary of Agriculture* v. *United States*, 350 U.S. 162 (1956) ; *St. Joe Paper Co.* v. *Atlantic Coast Line*, 347 U.S. 298 (1954) ; *Secretary of Agriculture* v. *United States*, 347 U.S. 645 (1954).

64. *Office Employees Union* v. *NLRB*, 353 U.S. 313 (1957) ; *NLRB* v. *Truck Drivers Union*, 353 U.S. 87 (1957) ; *NLRB* v. *Lion Oil Co.*, 352 U.S. 282 (1957) ; *Amalgamated Meat Cutters & Butchers* v. *NLRB*, 352 U.S. 153 (1956) ; *Leedom* v. *International Union*, 352 U.S. 145 (1956) ; *NLRB* v. *Truitt Mfg. Co.*, 351 U.S. 149 (1956) ; *NLRB* v. *Babcock & Wilson Co.* (3 cases), 351 U.S. 105 (1956) ; *NLRB* v. *Coca-Cola*, 350 U.S. 264 (1956) ; *Mastro Plastics Corp.* v. *NLRB*, 350 U.S. 270 (1956) ; *NLRB* v. *The Warren Co.*, 350 U.S. 107 (1955) ; *Brooks* v. *NLRB*, 348 U.S. 96 (1954) ; *Radio Officers' Union* v. *NLRB* (3 cases), 347 U.S. 17 (1954) ; *Howell Chevrolet Co.* v. *NLRB*, 346 U.S. 482 (1953) ; *NLRB* v. *Local Union No. 1229*, 346 U.S. 464 (1953).

65. John P. Frank, *The Marble Palace* (New York: Alfred A. Knopf, 1958), p. 148.

CHAPTER 3

DEMOCRACY

1. *Munn* v. *Illinois*, 94 U.S. 113, 134 (1877).

2. *Chicago, Milwaukee & St. P. Ry.* v. *Minnesota*, 134 U.S. 418 (1890), is the turning point.

3. Oliver Wendell Holmes, *Collected Legal Papers* (New York: Harcourt, Brace & Co., 1920), p. 184.

4. Arthur Twining Hadley, "The Constitutional Position of Property in America," *Independent*, LXIV (April 9, 1908), 834, 837.

5. *Lockner* v. *New York*, 198 U.S. 45, 75–76 (1905).

6. Robert H. Jackson, *The Struggle for Judicial Supremacy* (New York: Alfred A. Knopf, 1941), p. 72.

7. Dissenting opinion in *Connecticut Gen. Life Ins. Co.* v. *Johnson*, 303 U.S. 77, 85 (1938). See also *Wheeling Steel Corp.* v. *Glander*, 337 U.S. 562, 576 (1949).

8. Dissenting opinion in *Adamson* v. *California*, 332 U.S. 46, 48 (1947).

9. Dissenting opinion in *Hood* v. *Du Mond*, 336 U.S. 525, 551, note 2 (1949).

10. *Thomas* v. *Collins*, 323 U.S. 516, 529–30 (1945).

11. *Dennis* v. *United States*, 341 U.S. 494, 580 (1951).

12. See the *Gibony* case, below.

13. *Martin* v. *Struthers*, 319 U.S. 141, 152 (1943).

14. *AFL* v. *American Sash & Door Co.*, 335 U.S. 538, 556–57 (1949).

15. *West Va. Bd. of Ed.* v. *Barnette*, 319 U.S. 624, 650 (1943).

16. Id., at 646 and 666.

17. Cardozo spoke of the clash of "pretending absolutes," and long ago Chief Justice Marshall held that "when two [constitutional] principles came in conflict with each other, the court must give them both a reasonable construction, so as to preserve them both to a reasonable extent." *United States* v. *Burr*, 25 Fed. Cas. 38, 39, No. 14692e (D. Ky. 1807).

18. *AFL* v. *American Sash & Door Co.*, 335 U.S. 538, 553, 555 (1949).

19. *West Va. Bd. of Ed.* v. *Barnette*, 319 U.S. 624, 648–49 (1943).

20. *Dennis* v. *United States*, 341 U.S. 494 (1951). See Wallace Mendelson, "Clandestine Speech and the First Amendment," 51 Michigan Law Review 553 (1953).

21. See Aristotle, as set out in Charles McIlwain, *The Growth of Political Thought in the West* (New York: Macmillan Co., 1932) p. 88.

22. Mr. Justice Black has recently insisted, though not from the bench, that *within* its "area" freedom of speech (like some other basic liberties) is absolute. He recognizes, however, that the "scope" of its "area" is not clear. See Black, "The Bill of Rights," 35 New York University Law Review 865, 875 (1960).

23. Thus it is one thing for Mr. Justice Frankfurter to recognize that certain liberties come to the Court with a special "momentum of respect"; it is something quite different to buttress that respect with a presumption of invalidity for legislative law and use it as a substitute for judgment on the peculiar facts of a concrete case. See *Kovacs* v. *Cooper*, 336 U.S. 77, 95 (1949).

24. *Masses Publishing Co.* v. *Patten,* 244 Fed. 535, 540 (S.D. N.Y. 1917).

25. 341 U.S. 494 (1951).

26. "Can the Supreme Court Guarantee Toleration?" *New Republic,* XLIII (June 17, 1925), 85, 86, 87 (emphasis added).

27. 314 U.S. 252 (1941).

28. 354 U.S. 234 (1957).

29. Thomas Reed Powell, *Vagaries and Varieties in Constitutional Interpretation* (New York: Columbia University Press, 1956), p. 82.

30. Reproduced in Dilliard, *The Spirit of Liberty,* p. 218.

31. *Milk Wagon Drivers Union* v. *Meadowmoor Dairies,* 312 U.S. 287, 301–2 (1941).

32. *Terminiello* v. *Chicago,* 337 U.S. 1 (1949).

33. Quoted in Herman Pritchett, *Civil Liberties and the Vinson Court* (Chicago: University of Chicago Press, 1954), pp. 248–49.

34. 336 U.S. 490 (1949).

35. Reproduced in Dilliard, *op. cit.,* pp. 129–31.

36. Reproduced in Felix Frankfurter, *Of Law and Men* (New York: Harcourt, Brace & Co., 1956), pp. 213, 215.

37. *Cantwell* v. *Connecticut,* 310 U.S. 296, 303–4 (1940).

38. 319 U.S. 141 (1943).

39. Zachariah Chafee, *Free Speech in the United States* (Cambridge, Mass.: Harvard University Press, 1941), p. 407.

40. 341 U.S. 622 (1951).

41. *West Va. Bd. of Ed.* v. *Barnette,* 319 U.S. 624 (1943).

42. 343 U.S. 306 (1952).

43. 333 U.S. 203 (1948).

44. *Lochner* v. *New York,* 198 U.S. 45 (1905). See note 5, above, and related text.

45. "The Red Terror of Judicial Reform," *New Republic,* XL (October 1, 1924), 110, 113. See Felix Frankfurter, *Law and Politics* (New York: Harcourt, Brace & Co., 1939), p. 16.

46. *Louisiana ex rel. Francis* v. *Resweber,* 329 U.S. 459, 468 (1947).

47. *Osborn* v. *Ozlin,* 310 U.S. 53, 62 (1940).

48. *Lochner* v. *New York,* 198 U.S. 45, 76 (1905).

49. *Shaughnessy* v. *United States ex rel. Mezei,* 345 U.S. 206, 224 (1953).

50. Alpheus T. Mason, *Brandeis, A Free Man's Life* (New York: Viking Press, 1946), p. 569.

51. *Joint Anti-Fascist Com.* v. *McGrath,* 341 U.S. 123, 163–64 (1951).

52. *Louisiana ex rel. Francis* v. *Resweber,* 459 U.S. 349, 468 (1947).

53. *Adamson* v. *California,* 332 U.S. 46, 63 (1947).

54. *Malinski* v. *New York,* 324 U.S. 401, 417 (1945).

55. *Haley* v. *Ohio,* 332 U.S. 596, 603 (1948).

56. Id., at 602. Here will be found an example of Mr. Justice Frankfurter's self-analysis.

57. *Carter* v. *Illinois,* 329 U.S. 173 (1946).

58. *Uveges* v. *Pennsylvania,* 335 U.S. 437, 449–50 (1948).

59. *Foster* v. *Illinois,* 332 U.S. 134, 139 (1947). Of course, in this Mr. Justice Black goes beyond the original meaning of the Bill of Rights which contemplated merely that the accused had a *right to hire counsel.* See William Beaney, *The Right to Counsel in American Courts* (Ann Arbor: University of Michigan Press, 1955), pp. 27–44.

60. 351 U.S. 12 (1956).

61. *Alcorta* v. *Texas,* 355 U.S. 28 (1957); *Winters* v. *New York,* 333 U.S. 507 (1948); *Brown* v. *Topeka,* 347 U.S. 483 (1954). And see *Crooker* v. *California,* 357 U.S. 433 (1958).

62. See the Fifth, Sixth and Seventh amendments to the Constitution.

63. Nor, with respect to those cases in which a state recognizes a right to trial by jury, does there seem to be any particular magic in the traditional number of twelve jurors.

64. See *Betts* v. *Brady,* 316 U.S. 455 (1942). See note 59, above.

65. See *Wolf* v. *Colorado,* 338 U.S. 25 (1949).

66. See *Palko* v. *Connecticut,* 302 U.S. 319 (1937).

67. See *Adamson* v. *California,* 332 U.S. 46 (1947).

68. 287 U.S. 45 (1932).

69. 316 U.S. 455 (1942).

70. See *Bruno* v. *United States,* 308 U.S. 287 (1939); *Nardone* v. *United States,* 308 U.S. 338 (1939); *McNabb* v. *United States,* 318 U.S. 332 (1943); *Fisher* v. *United States,* 328 U.S. 463, 477 (1946); *Harris* v. *United States,* 331 U.S. 145, 155 (1947); *On Lee* v. *United States,* 343 U.S. 747, 758 (1952).

71. See Paul Freund, *On Understanding the Supreme Court* (Boston: Little, Brown & Co., 1949), pp. 22–25.

72. 338 U.S. 25 (1949).

73. John Holliday, *The Life of William, Late Earl of Mansfield* (London, 1797), p. 211.

74. See, for example, Mr. Justice Frankfurter's remarks in *West Va. Bd. of Ed.* v. *Barnette,* 319 U.S. 624, 646–47 (1943); *Harisiades* v. *Shaughnessy,* 342 U.S. 580, 596–98 (1952).

75. See, for example, Mr. Justice Black's position in *Trupiano* v. *United States,* 334 U.S. 699 (1948), and in *Wolf.*

76. *Zorach* v. *Clauson,* 343 U.S. 306 (1952).

77. *Adamson* v. *California,* 332 U.S. 46, 91–92 (1947).

78. Besides *Zorach* see *Tenney* v. *Brandhove,* 342 U.S. 367 (1951); *Wolf* v. *Colorado,* 338 U.S. 25 (1949); and compare *Ciucci* v. *Illinois,* 356 U.S. 571 (1958).

79. *FPC* v. *Natural Gas Pipeline,* 315 U.S. 575, 599, 600, note 4 (1942).

80. As suggested in chap. 2, Mr. Justice Frankfurter's "external standard" in case of doubt in *legislative* law is the legislative compromise. See also his approach in *Youngstown Sheet and Tube Co.* v.

Sawyer, 343 U.S. 579 (1952) and *Wolf* v. *Colorado*, 338 U.S. 25 (1949).

81. Reproduced in Frankfurter, *Of Law and Men*, pp. 31, 39–40.

82. *Dred Scott* v. *Sandford*, 19 Howard 393 (1857).

83. 100 U.S. 303 (1880) ; 100 U.S. 339 (1880).

84. 163 U.S. 537 (1896).

85. C. V. Woodward, *Reunion and Reaction* (Garden City, N.Y.: Doubleday & Co., 1956).

86. *Pollock* v. *Farmers' Loan & Trust Co.*, 157 U.S. 429 (1895) ; *United States* v. *E. C. Knight*, 156 U.S. 1 (1895) ; *In re Debs*, 158 U.S. 564 (1895).

87. The extra-party political alliance of the Bourbons was facilitated by an interregnum in our political party system. See Mendelson, "Judicial Review and Party Politics," 12 Vanderbilt Law Review 447 (1959).

88. *Missouri ex rel. Gaines* v. *Canada*, 305 U.S. 337 (1938).

89. See, for example, *Sweatt* v. *Painter*, 339 U.S. 629 (1950) ; *Sipuel* v. *Bd. of Regents*, 332 U.S. 631 (1948).

90. *Brown* v. *Bd. of Education of Topeka*, 347 U.S. 483 (1954) ; *Bolling* v. *Sharpe*, 347 U.S. 497 (1954).

91. Reproduced in Dilliard, *op. cit.*, pp. 15–16.

CHAPTER 4

FEDERALISM

1. James B. Bryce, *The American Commonwealth* (3d ed.; London: Macmillan Co., 1893), I, 562.

2. Harold J. Laski, *The American Democracy* (New York: Viking Press, 1948), p. 138.

3. Monrad Paulson, "The Persistence of Substantive Due Process in the States," 34 Minnesota Law Review 91 (1950).

4. *Our Sovereign States* (New York: Vanguard Press, 1949), p. vii.

5. *Uveges* v. *Pennsylvania*, 335 U.S. 437 (1948) ; *West Virginia* v. *Barnette*, 319 U.S. 624 (1943).

6. Article III, sec. 2.

7. Frankfurter, in *Lumbermen's Mutual Casualty Co.* v. *Elbert*, 348 U.S. 48, 54 (1955).

8. 16 Peters 1 (1842).

9. 304 U.S. 64 (1938).

10. 326 U.S. 99 (1945).

11. 356 U.S. 525 (1958).

12. 79 S. Ct. 2 (1958).

13. *Sutton* v. *Lieb*, 342 U.S. 402 (1952).

14. 319 U.S. 315 (1943).

15. *Merideth* v. *Winter Haven*, 320 U.S. 228 (1943).

16. 348 U.S. 48 (1945).

17. If prejudice against outsiders is a danger in state courts, why is it not equally a danger in federal courts? Like their state counterparts federal trial judges and juries come from the states in which they sit. Where there is in fact discrimination against outsiders the equal protection clause of the Fourteenth Amendment affords a federal remedy. This provision did not exist when diversity jurisdiction was established.

18. 337 U.S. 582 (1949).

19. *Prentis* v. *Atlantic Coast Line Co.*, 310 U.S. 573 (1940).

20. 312 U.S. 496 (1941).

21. 341 U.S. 341 (1951).

22. 353 U.S. 448 (1957).

23. Mr. Justice Black did not participate in the *Lincoln Mills* case, but he concurs in the majority view there expressed. See his position in *Association of Westinghouse Salaried Employees* v. *Westinghouse Electric Corp.*, 348 U.S. 437 (1955).

24. Id., at 498.

25. One element in the forces which led to the Taft-Hartley Act was the partially correct view that unions, unlike business corporations, were not suable as an entity.

26. Philip Kurland, "The Supreme Court and the Attrition of State Power," 10 Stanford Law Review 274, 296 (1958).

27. James Byrnes, "The Supreme Court Must Be Curbed," *U.S. News & World Report*, May 18, 1956.

28. *Brown* v. *Western Ry. of Alabama*, 338 U.S. 294 (1949).

29. See *Byrd* v. *Blue Ridge Rural Electric Cooperative.*

30. 337 U.S. 1 (1949).

31. 342 U.S. 485 (1952).

32. Article I, sec. 8.

33. *Gibbons* v. *Ogden*, 9 Wheaton 1 (1824).

34. See chap. 1.

35. *Polish National Alliance* v. *NLRB*, 322 U.S. 643 (1944).

36. 346 U.S. 441 (1953).

37. Article VI, sec. 2.

38. *Bethlehem Steel Co.* v. *N.Y. State Labor Relations Bd.*, 330 U.S. 767, 780 (1947).

39. *Cloverleaf Butter Co.* v. *Patterson*, 315 U.S. 148, 178 (1942).

40. 325 U.S. 538 (1943).

41. 350 U.S. 497 (1956).

42. See *Mesarosh* v. *United States*, 352 U.S. 1 (1956).

43. *Hood* v. *Du Mond*, 336 U.S. 525 (1949).

44. *Panhandle Eastern Pipeline Co.* v. *Michigan Public Service Com.*, 341 U.S. 329, 340 (1951).

45. Article I, sec. 8: "The Congress shall have power . . . to regulate commerce . . . among the several states. . . ." This has been treated

since Marshall's day as a grant of power to Congress and a restraint upon the states.

46. *Morgan* v. *Virginia*, 328 U.S. 373 (1946).

47. See Mr. Justice Black's views in *Hood* v. *Du Mond*, 336 U.S. 525 (1949).

48. This thought is spelled out in *Duckworth* v. *Arkansas*, 314 U.S. 390, 397 *et seq.* (1941).

49. *West Va. Bd. of Education* v. *Barnette*, 319 U.S. 624, 667 (1943).

50. *Hood* v. *Du Mond*, 336 U.S. 525, 564 (1949).

51. *Freeman* v. *Hewit*, 329 U.S. 249, 259 (1946).

52. Id., at 256.

53. *Union Brokerage Co.* v. *Jensen*, 322 U.S. 202, 211 (1944).

54. Id., at 210.

55. *Galveston, H. & S. A. Ry.* v. *Texas*, 210 U.S. 217, 227 (1908).

56. Alexander M. Bickel, *The Unpublished Opinions of Mr. Justice Brandeis* (Cambridge, Mass.: Belknap Press, 1957), pp. 115–18.

57. Even when the taxpayer is a resident of the taxing state, some of the burden or effects of the tax will fall upon outsiders at the other end of the interstate transaction.

58. *Prudential Insurance Co.* v. *Benjamin*, 328 U.S. 408 (1946).

59. 340 U.S. 349 (1951).

60. The dissenters also ignored another challenged provision of the ordinance which would have kept the Dean Milk Company out of Madison, even if the company had found it possible to acquire pasteurizing facilities within the five-mile limit. This other provision prohibited the sale of milk that had not come from approved sources within twenty-five miles of the city.

CHAPTER 5

JUSTICE AND DEMOCRACY

1. "The Common Law in the United States," 50 Harvard Law Review 25 (1936).

2. Frankfurter, "Judge Henry W. Edgerton," 43 Cornell Law Quarterly 161 (1957).

3. Notwithstanding the Dred Scott fiasco. See Mendelson, "Dred Scott's Case—Reconsidered," 38 Minnesota Law Review 16 (1953).

4. Quoted in Alpheus T. Mason, *Harlan Fiske Stone: Pillar of the Law* (New York: Viking Press, 1956), p. 469.

5. *Ibid.*, pp. 469–70.

6. *Whitney* v. *California*, 274 U.S. 357, 372 (1927). Mr. Justice Frankfurter's position in the *Terminiello* case rests on this principle.

7. That is, the things which because of their familiarity one can't help believing.

8. Quoted in Alpheus T. Mason, *Security through Freedom* (Ithaca, N.Y.: Cornell University Press, 1955), pp. 145–46.

9. Powell, *Vagaries and Varieties in Constitutional Law*, p. 82.

10. L. L. Jaffe, "Mr. Justice Jackson," 68 Harvard Law Review 940, 994–95 (1955).

11. T. Arnold, "Professor Hart's Theology," 73 Harvard Law Review 1298, 1311 (1960).

12. *Crooker* v. *California*, 357 U.S. 433, 441, 448 (1958).

13. *Murdock* v. *Pennsylvania*, 319 U.S. 105, 109 (1943).

14. *Prince* v. *Massachusetts*, 321 U.S. 158 (1944).

15. *West Va. State Board of Education* v. *Barnette*, 319 U.S. 624 (1943).

16. *Gibony* v. *Empire Storage & Ice Co.*, 336 U.S. 490 (1949).

17. *Local 10 etc.* v. *Graham*, 345 U.S. 192 (1953).

18. John P. Frank, *Mr. Justice Black: The Man and His Opinions* (New York: Alfred A. Knopf, 1948), p. 139.

19. See *U.S. News & World Report*, October 3, 1958.

20. Frank, *Mr. Justice Black*, p. 134.

21. *On Understanding the Supreme Court*, p. 65.

22. Morris Cohen, *Reason and Nature* (2d ed.; New York: Harcourt, Brace & Co., 1953), p. 11.

23. See, for example, *Adkins* v. *Children's Hospital*, 261 U.S. 525 (1923).

24. Walton Hamilton, quoted in Fred Rodell, *Nine Men* (New York: Random House, 1955), p. 271.

25. *Ibid.*

26. Frankfurter, *Of Law and Men*, p. 28.

27. Samuel Lubell, *Revolt of the Moderates* (New York: Harper & Bros., 1956), p. 239.

EPILOGUE—1966

1. Charles Reich, "Mr. Justice Black and the Living Constitution," 76. (My italics.) Harvard Law Review 673, 750 (1963).

2. *Bell* v. *Maryland*, 378 U.S. 226 (1964).

3. *Griswold* v. *Connecticut*, 85 S. Ct. 1678 (1965).

4. Id. 1702, 1704. Some may be excused for finding only "natural law" behind Mr. Justice Black's position in *Wesberry* v. *Sanders*, 376 U.S. 1 (1964), and *Reynolds* v. *Sims*, 377 U.S. 533 (1964), both decided only a few months before *Griswold*.

5. The "boxscores" issued annually by the Commission on Law and Social Action of the American Jewish Congress (mimeographed) reveal a marked shift in Mr. Justice Black's position on the Court. For years prior to the 1963 Term his "score" in favor of civil liberty was second only to that of Mr. Justice Douglas. In the 1963 and 1964 Terms he

dropped to third place. In the next two Terms he fell to the number five position. The 1967 Term found him in the seventh place.

Comes now Professor A. E. D. Howard—like Professor Reich (see note 1, above) an admiring former law clerk—insisting that Justice has never been an activist, that his recent stance is not a departure from, but a continuation of, a long-time dedication to the Rule of Law. "Mr. Justice Black: The Negro Movement and the Rule of Law," 50 Virginia Law Review 1030 (1967). No doubt Mr. Howard's analysis is quite compatible with the judge's *words*, just as Mr. Reich's view is quite compatible with the judge's *votes* (prior to the early 1960's).

Case Index

149

Union Brokerage Co. v. Jensen, 107

United States v. Burr, 48

United States v. E. C. Knight, 2, 75

United States v. Five Gambling Devices, 100

United States v. Hutcheson, 34, 35, 36

United States v. ICC, 31

United States v. Midwest Oil Co., 12

United States v. Morgan, 38

United States v. Southeastern Underwriters Assoc., 32

Uveges v. Pennsylvania, 68, 80

Vermilya-Brown v. Connell, 18

Wabash, St. Louis and Pacific Ry. v. Illinois, 2

Wesberry, v. Sanders, 132–34

West Virginia Bd. of Education v. Barnette, 47, 50, 62, 80, 89, 105, 122, 130

Western Union v. Lenroot, 19

Whitney v. California, 116

Wilkerson v. McCarthy, 23

Winters v. New York, 69

Wolf v. Colorado, 70, 71, 72, 73

Yates v. United States, 29

Youngstown Sheet & Tube Co. v. Sawyer, 9, 10, 11, 73, 110

Zorach v. Clauson, 63, 72, 73

Subject Index